CLIFFORD AND DAPHNE WEBB JEMMETT
A Historical Collection

By Merle Reid Clark

Copyright 2025, by Merle Reid Clark
ISBN: 978-1-7341924-7-6
Published by Cedar Creek Press, Boise, Idaho

Table of Contents

Introduction 4
Clifford Jemmett Family Tree 5
Cliff's Paternal Great Grandparents 8
Cliff's Paternal Great Grandparents 11
Cliff's Paternal Grandparents 13
Cliff's Maternal Great Grandparents 26
Cliff's Maternal Grandparents 28
Cliff's Parents 30
Daphne Webb Jemmett Family Tree 56
Daphne's Paternal Great Grandparents 58
Daphne's Great Grandparents 60
Daphne's Paternal Grandparents 62
Daphne's Maternal Great Grandparents 65
   Orderville 76
Daphne's Parents 81
   Delly and Martha's Marriage 86
   Martha's Homestead 87
   Back to Orderville 90
   The Move to Idaho 92
Clifford and Daphne Webb Jemmett 96
Early Years in Alridge 107
   The Kids Almost Grown 114
   After the Move to Blackfoot 119
   Five Simple Rules on How to be Happy, though Married 123
   Trapping and Hunting Stories 125
   The War Years 130
Burial Sites 145
Epilogue 146
Sources 146

Introduction

Along the Rivers was written by my mother, Alma Jemmett Reid. She was a painter as well as a writer, and we kids' homes are decorated with her artwork. When she started writing, I thought her time would be much better spent painting. Now I appreciate her tenacity to produce such a massive writing project. It was her mother, my grandmother, Daphne Webb Jemmett, who dreamed of writing a book, but as she aged and realized it would never be achieved, my mom accepted the challenge, took the information Grandma had gathered, and jumped in. I have been interested in history and our ancestors all my life. To have a reference book has been amazing. Mom wrote it all in longhand or on a typewriter, and gave it to my sister Kittie, who typed it into a computer. Mom wrote her book without seeing information by the click of a mouse or the ease of spell check and cut and paste. When she died, I found things she had written that she thought too trivial to use in her book. It was these notes that started my own journey.

I organized this information under main headings of Jemmett and Webb, and sub headings of each family group. I wanted things to be as close to the truth as possible, so I typed everything as it was written, only writing my own words to tie them together or make sense. I have noted the people that wrote something, (Alma wrote) and are *italicized*. Those individuals in our ancestral line are bolded.

Where I haven't specifically noted the writer, it is information I gathered by asking questions of my mother. I'm sure this isn't completely accurate, but it is my best effort.

I have a more complete family tree on ancestry.com, but for this manuscript, I only go to Cliff and Daphne's great grandparents. This is hopefully a small enough group that you can keep them straight in your mind. Keep returning to the tree if you lose your place. If there is a photo it is much easier to keep them straight in your mind.

I tried to keep things together that is about a particular person, event or subject. Chronological order is general.

I have written a book about my Reid ancestors, my father's side. This is about my mother's ancestors, the Jemmett book. I hope you find it interesting and correct to your recollections.

My sister Wendy Pratt has edited it, and my sister Becky Davis has mulled over it several times to find spelling and grammatical errors. Wendy's daughter Anna Lickley worked on formatting and my cousin Rick Just published it in the form you now see. Thanks everyone, I couldn't have dreamed it would come to this.

Clifford Jemmett Family Tree

Clifford Jemmett

Father
Henry Jemmett

Grandparents
Henry George (Harry) Jemmett

Great-Grandparents
William Lewington Jemmett

Mary Ann Browning

Eliza Elliot

William Elliot

Eliza Nichols

Mother
Elizabeth (Lizzie) Goddard

Grandparents
Eli Goddard

Great- Grandparents
Martin Goddard

Electra Lucretia Sanders

Amelia Thorpe

William Thorpe

Elizabeth Sims

Clifford's paternal ancestors were Mormon converts from England. For generations they lived in the Faversham area of Kent County, England. These folks had boats and made their living on the sea.

My sisters and I went to England and Scotland in 2014. We started at the bottom of England and worked our way to the northernmost islands of Scotland where our Reid ancestors came from. The shipping town of Faversham, on the North Sea east of London, was the first day of our "trip of a lifetime." Our tour guide took us to the area where our Jemmett ancestors lived. We saw the waterway where they would take their boats out to the ocean. When we were there the tide was out and the boats were sitting in mud. When the tide comes in, the boats can be floated out into the harbor. We saw the buildings of Brent Town where our ancestors would have lived.

Brent Town opposite side of Faversham Creek

Our tour guide had contacted our relative, Dawn Jemmett Emery, who lived locally (with umbrella) and arranged for her to meet us. Her family had stayed in England and she shared her belief that the people who went across the ocean were of stronger stock than the ones that stayed. We had tea in a home that was once a bakery run by our ancestors in the 19th century.

Faversham

Cliff's Paternal Great Grandparents
William Lewington and Mary Ann Browning Jemmett

William Lewington Jemmett
Feb 24, 1811 - Oct 10, 1864

Mary Ann Browning Jemmett
April 3, 1796 - April 28, 1883

Children

William Henry	1835 - 1914
Henry George (Harry)	1837 - 1904
Edward	1839 - 1859
Julia Jane	1840 - 1925
Rosina Kathleen	1843 - 1934

Mary Ann was married at 16 to Nicholas Mears. He was a constable in Kent County, England. They had 7 children and were expecting another, when he, only 33 at the time, was murdered in a riot. He, his brother, and another man went to arrest Sir William and his followers at Rosendin Farm. Nicholas had a premonition that something awful was going to happen, but he didn't want to leave his brother in a bind. Sir William met them at the door and when Nicholas said that he was the constable, Sir William shot him point blank.

At least one of Mary Ann's Mears's children, Frances Ann Curtis, came to America. She was most likely a Mormon convert too, because she settled in Utah.

Mary Ann married again at 37 to William Jemmett who was 23 years old. The Jemmetts were converted to Mormonism around 1848 when Harry was 14. They hosted missionaries in their home and held meetings there. William was a strictly righteous man. He would work extra hard on Saturday so he wouldn't have to work on Sunday. The family wouldn't even cook meals on Sunday. When daughter Julia Jane, her husband Thomas Potts, and their daughter left for America, William said the only way he could stand for her to go was to believe that there was a life after this, and that he would see her again.

Mary Ann was a very industrious woman. She kept every small scrap of cloth to work into quilts and she ironed everything, even underwear and rags. Mary Ann was a beautiful seamstress, making tiny, even stitches by hand. She also liked to knit.

William had been the master of a sailing barge named the *Good Design*. He taught all his sons to work on the sea. His occupation was mainly that of an oyster dredger, but his boat also hauled freight.

Faversham was a gun powder manufacturing town and a seaport. William was hauling gunpowder up the Thames River when his ship blew up. It isn't known what set the powder off, but his ship, a second ship, and the storage building all blew up. The accident killed everyone on board and in the storage building. The town was torn up and even windows in London were broken from the blast. The accident was most likely caused by someone smoking. This accident was the impetus for more stringent safety regulations.

William had a little dog he always took with him on the boat. The family was in the living room when they heard scratching at the door, like the dog would do when they were returning home each day. Three times they went to the door but noone was there. Later they learned this was when the ship blew up.

When Mary Ann was 69, she made her way to America with her remaining daughter Rosina. I found evidence of them sailing on the ship *Hudson*, which left from London, unknown date. They traveled west on the Miner Atwood wagon train Company in 1865, left Wyoming, Nebraska, July 31, and arrived in Salt Lake valley on Nov 8.

Mary Ann spent her last years helping Jane raise her family. She died peacefully as she lived, at 86 years of age. She is buried at Heber City, Utah.

Children of William and Mary Ann Jemmett

William Henry
Aug 24, 1835 - July 11, 1914

William and his wife were the first to immigrate to America in 1857. He lived in the Missouri area for the rest of his life.

Henry George (Harry)
Nov 3, 1837 - Dec 27, 1904

Harry was a sailor by profession and became very dissatisfied at the treatment of the common people by those in power.

Edward
1839 - 1859
Washed overboard in the ocean

Julia Jane
Dec 17, 1840 - Sept 23, 1925
    Married Thomas Potts and came to the U.S. June 13, 1862, arriving at New York. They came as Mormon converts and lived in Utah all their lives. Julia's mother, Mary Ann, spent her later years with this family.

Rosina Kathleen
Sept 25, 1843 - March 3, 1934
    Rosina accompanied Mary Ann to America and Utah, then settled in Montana. In the Bingham County Book it states that in the 1870's Rosina married Charles O. Johnson. They operated the Sand Hole Stage north of Hamer, Idaho. Her mother Mary Ann was there in 1880. This was the first time the Jemmetts were known to be in Bingham County which was much larger than present day.

Cliff's Paternal Great Grandparents

William and Eliza Nichols Elliot

No pictures

William Elliott	**Eliza Nichols Elliot**
Aug 18, 1811 – 1880	May 21, 1815 – 1880

Children

Eliza	1843 - 1912
William	1846 - ?
Fredrick	1849 - 1920
Henry	1850 - 1917
Kenny	1851 - ?
Orson	1857 - 1859

(Daphne wrote) *William Elliott was a captain of a fleet of dredges working the oyster beds in British waters. He was working for a company of oyster merchants who were in competition with others who would hesitate at nothing to do each other "dirt." They had their own dredging grounds and some way they maneuvered William's boat into illegal waters. He was imprisoned and made to work on a treadmill for a long time.*

(From Google search) *Treadmills were originally torture devices meant to break the mind, body and spirit of English prisoners. Two hundred years ago, these were invented in England as a prison rehabilitation device. It was meant to cause the incarcerated to suffer and learn from their sweat.*

William's wages being cut off, his wife and daughter were forced to glean in the wheat fields for food. He was never able to think of England without bitterness.

Children of William and Eliza Elliot

Eliza
Sept 2, 1843 – Feb 17, 1912

William
Feb 16, 1846 - ?
   There is a family story of 17-year-old William Elliot being captured by the Indians. The story goes that he escaped and made his way back to England, and later returned to

live in America. I can't find any evidence of this, and I can't find him on any English or American censuses.

Fredrick
Dec 25, 1849 – Feb 2, 1920
    Fred Elliot is living with widowed Eliza in Shelley in the 1910 census.

Henry
Dec 2, 1850 - 1917
    Both Fred and Henry lived in Idaho a long time.

Kenny
1851 - ?

Orson
1857 – 1859

    Eliza came across the ocean on the ship *Antarctic*, boarding on May 23, 1863 and landed in New York on July 10. I found the names of William Elliot 51, and wife Eliza 48, and their sons, Henry 12, Fredrick 13, and William 17, their daughter Eliza Jemmett 20, her daughter, Emma, infant and Martha Nichols 75, Eliza Elliot's mother.
    Also on the list of passengers was William Jemmett 27, Harry's brother who lived in America by that time. William must have been in England visiting and accompanied them on the ship. He probably made his way back home to Missouri from New York where they landed. It is fun to know that William would have helped his brother's pregnant wife Eliza and young Emma on the journey.
    The wagon train was unidentified but went across the Plains in 1863.

Cliff's Paternal Grandparents
Henry George (Harry) and Eliza Elliot Jemmett

Henry George (Harry) Jemmett
Nov 3, 1837 - Dec 27, 1904

Eliza Elliot Jemmett
Sept 2, 1843 - Feb 17, 1912

Children

Emma	1861 – 1933
twin stillborn daughters	died on the trail west
William (Bill)	1865 – 1925
Eliza	1866 – 1957
Henry	**1871 - 1948**
Molly Blanch	1873 – 1944
Fredrick	1880 – 1883
Charlotte	1876 – 1924
Edward	1881 – 1907
George	1883 – 1884
Eva	1885 – 1891
Howard	1890 - 1968

These grandparents moved to the Shelley area in their later years so Cliff knew them very well.

(Harry wrote) *If I hadn't of left to come to America the 3 of June 1864, I probably would have been with my father on that fateful day he was killed. Eliza had left England May 23, 1863, with her parents, William and Eliza Nichols Elliott. I hated to see her and our little girl Emma go, as Eliza was pregnant at the time. But I knew she would be in good hands with her parents. We didn't have enough money for all to go, so I had to stay and earn my fare.*

My voyage crossing the ocean was an experience I'll never forget. There were 900 Latter Day Saints, consisting of English, Scotch, Welch, Danish, Scandinavian, Swiss. There also were 200 Irish, whom were partitioned off from the Saints. We saints went to steerage which meant we descended through a trap door to quarters below deck. We slept on large shelves fastened to the ship's sides. We ate at long tables, for those who were able to eat. Our meals consisted mainly of salt beef, salt pork, rice and hard tack of ship's biscuits. We had to break the biscuits open with a hammer. Each person was given a linen bag to hold these articles and at a specified time be at the commissary to receive the allotment of fresh water.

44 days we were cramped and huddled like animals. Measles broke out and nine little children died, only to go to a watery grave. One of the saints, George Careless wrote the hymn, "The Morning Breaks and Shadows Flee." To cheer we weary Saints. On July 16, we sighted the shore line of America. Upon landing we were placed in the Castle Gardens. The place was not only rat infested, but we immigrants ourselves were covered with body lice and stinking from the odor of the overcrowded ship's hold. We were then loaded on railroad cars. They were neither clean nor comfortable. Delays of all kinds were met due to the Civil War, bridges and railroad tracks were torn out by the confederate armies. Finally at Saint Joseph, Missouri, we were placed on a Missouri River boat that took us to Winter Quarters, Nebraska, on August 6. For two weeks we lived in a little bush shelter awaiting preparations for the journey over the plains.

The journey was wearisome and hard, walking most of the way. Some days traveling only two hours a day. We all suffered from cold and exposure and shortages of food.

Both Eliza and I were overjoyed when we were reunited. It had been over one year and about 5 months since we had last seen one another.

There are several different stories of how Harry made his way west. Eliza was heard to say "He rode across the plains on horseback with his cousin, Tom Potts." Tom was his brother-in-law. He wasn't on the ship manifest. Another story is he arrived at New York, bought a horse and rode across the plains with an oxen train with his brother-in-law. Neither are close to his own story above.

Eliza was living with a widow in Utah. When Harry arrived, he moved in too. He would take the widow's horses and wagon and haul wood from the mountains to sell and help with the expenses. He sold his horse and bought a cow which provided milk for the group. She grew increasingly friendly, and would often tell Eliza, "You go to bed and get your rest. I'll wait up for Harry." It went well until the widow thought the arrangement should be made more permanent, meaning Harry should take her as a second wife. When he refused, they had to find other housing in the middle of the winter.

The cow had to be sold because the people of the community thought he should have accepted the widow's request, and refused to sell him hay for the animal. Harry built a dugout for them to live in across Cache Valley at the site where Hyrum was being organized into a community. Times were very tough and the family survived on a diet of roasted potatoes.

(Eliza Elliot Jemmett wrote) *First, I would like to let you know I was the only girl in a family with five brothers, four younger than I, so I learned responsibility young.*

I, too, will never forget the experience on the ocean coming to America and especially the trip across the plains, where our twin girls were born and died. It was terrible to know I had to leave them out there with the possibility of animals devouring them. The wagon train wouldn't stop long enough for me to see them buried so my brothers Fred and Henry stayed behind to bury them. They then had to walk to catch up with the wagons.

When Harry, as I and everyone called him, arrived that first winter we lived in a dug out with nothing much to eat but potatoes. In the spring we rented a piece of land and raised a large crop of Lucerne seed. The warehouse where we stored our seed burned so our dreams went up in smoke. We moved from Beaver Dam area where we were farming back to the town site of Collinston. It was there Harry worked on the railroad. He operated a livery stable and a saloon, while I kept busy running a boarding house, and the first Post Office in the area, taking in washing and ironing for others as well as caring for our seven children, Emma, William, Eliza, Henry, Molly, Charlotte and Edward. Besides the twins, we lost two little boys, Fredrick and George, and little 6-year-old Eva who died as a result of a fire.

Harry ran race horses for a hobby and was elected Constable in Collinston Precinct in 1890. It was quite a responsibility to keep peace in that growing western town. It was that same year, when I was 47 years old, that I gave birth to our 13th child whom we named Howard.

In 1892 when Howard was two years old, my son Henry and his wife Elizabeth took care of him as I had the opportunity given me by the church to go to Salt Lake for two years to study nursing under Dr. Maggie Shipp. I received a certificate in Midwifery and nursing April 1884 (This date is wrong). The first of April 1895 I received a license from the Board of Medical Examiners to practice Medicine and Obstetrics, five months before I turned 52 years old.

One day a team of horses Harry was driving bolted and run. Harry was thrown from the wagon and suffered a severe back and head injury. He was never able to work after that. Even though he was a semi-invalid, he was tremendous help to me. He chopped and carried in the wood for our stove. It was quite a distance from the well, but he packed our water in two buckets attached to a yolk around his neck. He also took care of two cows, my horse and buggy, and kept the stable spotlessly clean.

Children of Harry and Eliza Jemmett

Emma
Nov 24, 1861 – Jan 31, 1933

Since Emma and her family played such an important part in Henry and Lizzie's life, I have included more information about her.

(Alma wrote) *Daphne thought "Auntie Em" was a really great person. When Les, just older than me, was born, our whole family stayed with her and the doctor came there for the delivery. She helped Daphne and Cliff out sometimes by taking care of them and their kids. Daphne thought of her as "an old dear."*

Emma married Bill Twitchell in 1880 in Collinston, Utah

Emma's Children with Bill Twitchell

Bill, Eliza, Bertha, Fred and Bill (Sr.) Twitchell (no photo of George)

(Alma wrote) *George Twitchell, Cliff's best friend and cousin, was killed in the prime of his life, probably in his twenties. Guns were a prized possession in those days and George was a lover of guns. There was a gun hung in a holster on a wagon. George took it from the holster and looked it over to his satisfaction. When he was putting it back in the holster, it went off and killed him instantly.* When Cliff had his first son, he named him George in his honor.

Emma's husband Bill Twitchell had a drinking problem. Emma took to washing clothes for the freighters to feed and clothe her kids. She finally left Bill and moved in with Henry and Lizzie and family.

It was hard on everyone to have Emma's big family added to the small cabin. This is during the time Lizzie had baby Cliff and had the accident to her foot that you will read about later.

Henry was chopping wood. He wanted Emma's boys to carry the wood to the house. When they didn't do it quickly enough, he spanked them. This made Emma mad enough to look for another home.

This brings George Edward (Scaley) Monroe into our family tree.

One winter he froze his ears and his skin scaled off, hence "Scaley." Another less sympathetic relative simply said, "If you looked at Scaley you knew why."

George was born in New York and was of Scottish descent. He left home at an early age and worked as a freighter on the Great Lakes. George only lasted a short time on the water, his violent temper led to his hitting another man with a Marlin spike. He was only 14 and thought he had killed the man so he fled and lived as a fugitive for 20 years. He drifted across the United States and finally settled in Cedar Creek where he was getting his squatter rights on some ground. Henry Jemmett was close by working for Bill Twitchell, and started working for George. George was much older, but they were fast friends having much in common, particularly practical jokes.

(Alma wrote) *Scaley worked in Blackfoot to raise capital by tending bar or running a game at the gambling tables and was something of a mystery to most folks. Henry and George (Scaley) became friends and eventually partners. They built a cabin and corrals on the claim, taking herd stock from people in the valley to pasture along Cedar Creek. Henry tended the stock there.*

DeLoris Henscheid is an old family friend and a descendent of Emma's son, Fred Twitchell. She has contributed to George Monroe's story.

(DeLoris wrote) *He was the ultimate persona of a gambler and it was that gambling quirk of fate that brought this solemn, tempestuous, sometimes kindly, stranger to Cedar Creek at the vulnerable time of Emma Twitchell's life.*

Emma's kids said that she jumped from the frying pan into the fire when she married Scaley. "She *went from one ornery drunk to another."*

George and Emma married in 1895. (Alma wrote) *Scaley and Henry had a practical joke relationship, first one, then the other would pay back. Henry was never so careless of consequences as Scaley. When Scaley and Emma were married, Henry said. "Well at last, I'm really getting even with you."*

Scaley's temper was legendary. One time Emma was cooking for company. Something made George mad and he gathered the tablecloth, with dishes and food and dumped the mess out the door.

Emma's Children with George (Scaley) Monroe

Caddie
June 21, 1897 – March 14, 1983

Caddie fell into the spring. George pulled her out and went to beating on her chest. Emma looking on begged him to stop abusing her tiny body. But George continued until finally Caddie took a breath.

Walter
1899 – 1900

This baby is confused with the Jemmett baby. They both are named Walter, and are not buried with their parents. This baby is buried in Harry and Eliza's plot. I think it might be as simple as the parents didn't have a plot so he was buried with relatives that had room in theirs. Another mystery we'll never solve.

Belle
July 14, 1902 – Oct 8, 1968

Emma   Belle   Caddie above Scaley

(Daphne wrote) *After Emma's illness (?) it was almost impossible for her to do without the drug (morphine) given to her to ease the pain. George (Emma's son from her previous marriage) at one time would peddle bread his mother baked in Idaho Falls to get money for morphine, so Scaley wouldn't know.*

When Scaley found out, he said "I'd sooner see her dead than a dope fiend." However, with the help of everybody it was finally conquered. George was patient but firm. Pop (Cliff) thinks it was his help that cured her.

(Daphne wrote) *Scaley had increasingly bad headaches and went completely blind several years before Emma died. However, when Emma became violently ill, it was hard to realize he was blind, for he did what was necessary, instinctively without error.*

Henry was living in Mud Lake. One morning he was eating breakfast when he happened to glance out the window. There was his sister Emma, walking up the path towards him. His son Russell came into the house later to find Henry still sitting at the table, white and shaken. He was concerned and asked him what was wrong. Henry answered him with "Emma is dead." He soon found out that he was right.

Continuing Harry and Eliza Jemmett's Children

Twin daughters
June 1863
Stillborn on the Plains

William (Bill)
July 31, 1865 - Feb 19, 1925

William married Nellie. Nellie was a tiny 4'10" woman that weighed about 89 lbs. Bill was as tall as she was short. He could hold his arm out and she could walk under it. She never raised her voice, never said a bad thing. She could play any instrument and sing, and Bill played the accordion so they had a lot of fun with music.

Henry Jemmett and his brother Bill homesteaded and had cabins on Cedar Creek. Bill Jemmett worked for Sam Borup. Bill later worked on the railroad in Evanston, Wyoming, then back to Shelley and Mud Lake.

Bill had a son Bill who in turn had sons Bill and Fred. Fred's daughter was Shirley Lott who was interested in genealogy and Mom had contact with.

Eliza
Nov 30, 1866 - Oct 29, 1957
Eliza married Frederic L Vandooger.

Henry
Mar 20, 1871 – Dec 19, 1948

Molly Blanch
May 10, 1873 - Feb 5, 1944
Molly married Howard Beuginon.

Fredrick
Feb 19, 1880 - 1883
Died at 3 of an accidental poisoning

Charlotte
Oct 31, 1876 - Feb 8, 1924

Charlotte (Dottie) became a registered nurse and assisted Eliza in her work.

(Daphne wrote) *Married John Sanders, who was a perfect heel. When Henry and Lizzie were in Collinston for Elsie's birth, Sanders stole a 20-dollar gold piece Henry had given his mother for his family's expenses. Sanders went to Salt Lake and had a big time. The only thing they knew it was spent on was he brought their little girl, Nina, a little red rocking chair. Later he forged a 13 dollar and a 9 dollar check which Henry paid.*

Edward
Jan 6, 1881 - Apr 29, 1907

Cliff slept in the top story of the tiny house with this uncle Ed when he went to school in the winters. He was an alcoholic. Another good friend that Cliff lost.

(Didn't recognize the handwriting) *Henry Jemmett told me about his bother Edward who was supposed to have committed suicide, but the family never believed it. His wife had been stepping out on him; he went to Idaho Falls to see this man in a saloon. They went into a back room where the man said Ed shot himself by putting the gun is his mouth. (The man later married his wife and adopted his son).*

Ed's sister Molly said Ed appeared to her after his death and said he couldn't rest until they put his eye in his head. The Ghost indicated it was in the cuff of his left pant leg. She went to the undertaker and they found it there.

George
1883 – 1884

Eva
1885 – 1891
Eva died at 6 years old in a fire.

Howard
July 4, 1890 - Jan 20, 1968

Life in Utah for Harry and Eliza

Harry was a saloon keeper, had a livery stable and did freighting business. When he got his citizenship papers, he filed to homestead 80 acres near Collinston. On Aug 4, 1890, Harry was named constable in the Collinston Precinct and could settle arguments without the use of a gun. He was afraid he would lose his temper and would shoot someone. Here they manned a stage station and boarding house. This is where they would stay and raise a big family.

Besides their many children, Harry and Eliza raised two other girls, Annie Madsen and Lizzie Goddard. We'll read about Lizzie, who became a daughter-in-law, in the next section. Eliza said these girls were a great comfort to her in her later years.

Harry didn't take naturally to farming but he persevered and finally had a bumper crop of Lucerne (alfalfa) seeds. They stored the seed in a warehouse. The Jemmetts at last faced a future free of financial worries. They built a new home on the expectation of a good price, but the warehouse burned down, and all their lovely dreams went up in smoke. This was a financial blow from which they never fully recovered.

(Daphne wrote) *A wholesale liquor dealer went to the farm fishing, and talked Harry into putting a saloon in on the farm to accommodate the hunters and fishermen. He did this but sold so much liquor on credit that the dealer got control of the farm for the mortgage of three thousand dollars. He had many times that amount on the books but could not collect. That is how he lost his homestead.*

(Daphne wrote) *The Indians liked and respected Harry. They said he was "Big! Brave! Strong!"*

(Daphne wrote) *Henry told me how he and his brother Will used to wrestle with the Indian boys. The redskin children would form an immense circle to watch. When one of the Jemmett brothers would succeed in throwing an Indian, the others would whoop and holler as if it was a very good joke.*

(Daphne wrote) *One day when Harry was away freighting, a big Indian came to the house and asked to be fed. Eliza fed him, feeling frightened but tried not to show it. The Indian sensing her fear asked where Harry was. She told him that he was in a nearby field. The Indian laughed and said, "Me know Harry Jemmett. He goes town. Me see him. Me see dog Rover." Eliza was speechless but to her relief the Indian went on, "No be fraid, Me no hurt Harry squaw. Me pike away." and he left.*

(Daphne wrote) *The winter before the historic Bear River Massacre, they (Harry and Eliza) lived on a farm just across Bear River from where the Indians were camped. My Father-in-law Henry, from whom I gathered these details, told me that the Indians' camp was stretched along the river for miles. (Collinston is 37 miles from the Preston Bear River Massacre Monument.)*

The soldiers questioned Harry about the Indians behavior and he told them that they had given him no trouble. He always thought that a little diplomacy could have averted the terrible battle.

Some Indian children, orphaned by the battle, were found in an adjacent field. After a few years, one of these orphans called Hammon came to live with the Jemmetts. He stayed with them for several years. However, he seemed to have a weakness for stealing and destroying property of the whites who he did not like. Harry was continually getting him out of trouble.

(Alma wrote) *There was a neighbor man who treated Hammon especially badly. Hammon beat him up and stole his wagon and cattle. He brought these things to the Jemmett home and claimed they were his own. Harry knew this could not possibly be true. He returned them then paid off his fines. He told Hammon that that was the last time he would get him out of trouble. Harry always thought that his attitude towards the whites stemmed from what he had suffered at their hands and that he was to be pitied more than censured.*

I don't know if the Jemmetts ran the Hampton Ford Stage Station, but they did run a boarding house close to the station. My sisters and I drove to Collinston one day and found the barn which must have served as the station. It had big high doors on each end that would allow a stagecoach to enter and exit without turning around. The big, beautiful, stone house next door may have been Harry and Eliza's boarding house. It is now rented out as a venue for wedding parties.

I was hoping someone would be there to ask questions but there was no information other than the following I got from the internet.

Regular stage stations were every 10 miles, more substantial stations would be made every 80 miles for the passengers to spend the night. The Hampton station was the first overnight station from Salt Lake. The large hotel, made of native limestone 2 feet thick, had 18 rooms for guests. There the passengers would enjoy an evening meal, bed and breakfast the next morning for 35 cents.

After the passengers would disembark with their luggage, the stage would pull in the big double doors of the barn and would pull through as they left the next morning.

(DeLoris Henscheid wrote) *Harry Jemmett's fall from the wagon was serious. At first they thought he would not recover from the accident. Concerned that she would be widowed, Eliza went to the Brigham Court house and it was recorded that Harry had turned all of his personal property over to her. In August of the next year, Harry himself signed a quit claim deed that verified the same. The property included the house, saloon building, stable and other buildings near the Collinston station, four mares and colts and one stable horse named Prince, five cows, three calves and one single buggy and harness.*

(DeLoris wrote) *Eliza was trying to decide just what she should do next. She and Harry were an extremely close, practical couple, who looked life squarely in the face. They had worked hard together to support their large family, but Harry's health had been declining ever since his fall from the wagon. He began to have frequent blackouts and his strength and stamina were waning. Eliza was worried about her husband and she knew she had to do something more to help support the family*

She sent her two-yr-old son Howard with Lizzie when she went to Idaho to marry Eliza's older son Henry.

Eliza took a midwifery course offered by the Mormon Church in Salt Lake City. She got her certificate of Midwifery and Nursing in 1892. The certificate states:

This is to certify that Mrs. Eliza Jemmett has attended my entire course of lectures, and passed successful examinations upon the subject of Midwifery and Nursing. With great pleasure I recommend her as efficiently qualified to practice.
Signed Maggie C. Shipp M. D.

She didn't see Howard until Lizzie brought him back to Collinston for the birth of her first child, Cliff. Lizzie was able to return to Henry in a month or so.

Soon Eliza was traveling around the country delivering babies in her buggy pulled by her reliable horse, Prince. She delivered babies for 5 years around Collinston, Utah.

Life in Shelley

After the children were married and living in Idaho, Eliza and Harry wanted to move closer to them. In 1900, they moved to the Shelley area with their sons Edward, about 19, and Howard 9.

(Russell wrote) *Emma was thrilled to have her parents close once again and her brothers, Henry and Bill prepared a small house for the folks and their younger children. All the Jemmett, Twitchell and Monroe grandkids loved the warmth and kindness of their grandfather; the young uncles were great fun; but the pride they had for "Doctor Grandmother" was most cherished. Until their own closing days, all that remembered her shared memories of Eliza Jemmett traveling the countryside in her horse drawn buggy, sometimes puffing on a little corn cob pipe to ease her asthma, but always on her way to help bring new life, bid farewell to the old or simply relieve pain with the gentle touch for those somewhere in between.*

(Alma wrote) *After this move, she was the only doctor between Blackfoot and Idaho Falls. During those years she was devoted to her patients, she brought 100's of babies into the world and was appreciated and loved by families up and down the Snake River Valley.*

Henry and Lizzie's younger children, Frank and Eva, were born in Shelley after Harry and Eliza moved there. Russell was born after Eliza died.

Eliza would receive 15 dollars for a baby, or sometimes vegetables, meat or stitchery. She would never refuse to treat someone that didn't have the money. She once graciously received a bushel basket of apples when she had an orchard full at home.

The Shelley Pioneer newspaper gave many accounts of the babies Eliza delivered. One reads *"Mrs. Jemmett says Idaho's baby crop is unfailing and that the present prospects for a bumper winter crop is excellent in all directions."* My sister Janene found a snippet in the *Shelley Pioneer*, a reprint of what was happening in 1910 from the files. *Mrs. Jemmett delivered a baby girl in Firth and a bouncing baby boy the next day.*

(Russell wrote) *Those that remember her, see the one-horse buggy and a small gentle woman wrinkled and gray with an ever-ready smile as warm and friendly as sunshine on a cold December day.*

Eliza took out citizenship papers in Blackfoot. In the Declaration of Intent May 7, 1908, Eliza Jemmett was described as 62 years, occupation nurse, 5'6", wt. 125 lbs., brown hair and blue eyes.

Eliza's license forbid taking pay for any sort of medical service except that having to do with childbirth. She was often asked to help people in need of assistance, and she always did all she could, never turning anyone away who needed her help.

Showing she did more than deliver babies is the following 1953 statement written, signed and given to Mildred Jemmett, who was married to one of Eliza's grandsons, George. *"I here-by wish to pay tribute to a noble woman, who I got acquainted with when I was a young man, through service she rendered to me in sickness. I will always remember it was in the person of Mrs. Jemmett who was a practical nurse and midwife.*

I had taken an attack of inflammation of the bowels they called it then. I was very bad for a week and doctors didn't seem to know what to do for me at least what they did do, didn't do me any good. I got so bad that I bloated and was in awful pain, and I figured I was about to pass in my checks.

My mother had heard of a lady living in Shelley who hadn't lived there very long, who was very good in sickness and insisted on my father going after her, which he did.

She came in and looked at me and said, "you are very sick." She didn't need to tell me for when I would close my eyes, I could see small objects like birds flying overhead in the room, seemed to be full of them, spirits I suppose.

"Well," she said to mother "get a pan on the stove with water in it as warm as possible and your turpentine and put three or four tablespoonsful in the water." And when it got hot, they went to work and rang out hot cloths and laid them on my side and changed them every two minutes all night long for at least eight hours. The next morning their hands were nearly blistered and my side was as well. I was feeling one hundred percent better though very weak. I continued to get better and in a few days was up and around but was ailing for six months.

In a week or two my side peeled off and was purple for a year.

I have told this to many Doctors, long since this happened, and they all say if my appendix had ruptured in those days, there was only one case in a hundred that one would recover.

Well, after this I was married and raised a family and she was my family doctor and waited on my wife for at least four babies.

F. A. Wadsworth, 526 I Street, Idaho Falls

When Dr. Cutler came to the area, Eliza gladly gave up her practice.

Harry and Eliza's Final Days

Cliff said his grandfather was a great old fellow. He was one who saved everything, with the thought that it might come in handy later on. Cliff remembered once when his grandfather picked up a little square of wood. Looking it over, he said, "Maybe I can make a good paddle to grease the wagon out of this." Then he put it away carefully on the shelf in his shed.

Lizzie was at Harry and Eliza's in Shelley when she had Frank. Cliff and Henry had come to see the new baby but left again to do chores in the hills. Eliza had been out on a call so spent the night away from home. Lizzie heard Harry singing as he went to bed, but the next morning he didn't get up to start the fire. When Eliza came back, she knew he must have died in his sleep. Howard rode to the Cove on the Blackfoot River to tell Henry and Cliff the sad news.

Emma Monroe was living in New York with Scaley, Caddie and George Twitchell. She had a disturbing dream in which she saw her dad dancing around his coffin. Scaley tried to dismiss it as only a dream, but Emma knew that she would be getting a telegram the next day telling of her father's death. Caddie remembered walking for hours around Lake Erie with her upset mother. Emma did receive that feared telegram the next day.

Sometime after Harry died, Henry was at the Cove when he saw his dad and other people on the other side of the river. The others stayed on that side but his dad came over to talk to him. After a time, his dad told Henry that the others were waiting for him and he had to go.

Eliza was accompanied by Annie Madsen, the other girl she raised like Lizzie, to Evanston, Wyoming to stay with her son until the weather warmed up again. She peacefully died at the age of 69. She is buried in the old section of the Hillcrest Cemetery at Shelley.

The *Shelley Pioneer* printed the following tribute in her obituary. *"If a pleasant death is the greatest known reward for a long, honorable and useful life, she has that reward. She was respected by all."*

Cliff's Maternal Great Grandparents
William and Elizabeth Sims Thorpe

no picture

William Thorpe
Aug 19, 1814 – May 8, 1863

Elizabeth Sims Thorpe
Jan 8, 1816 – Oct 19, 1889

Children

William	Aug 22, 1836 – Feb 1, 1852
Martha	Feb 26, 1838 – Dec 28, 1912
John Horatio	Mar 1, 1840 – Sept 11, 1895
Samuel	May 20, 1842 – March 29, 1901
Thomas	May 29, 1844 – June 6, 1908
Mary Ann	March 28, 1845 – May 8, 1850
Amelia	**May 31, 1846 – Apr 8, 1887**
Ephraim	Apr 4, 1850 – Dec 10, 1870
Joseph	Feb 12, 1852 – Mar 10, 1932
Elizabeth Jane	Aug 23, 1854 – Nov 2, 1931
Alma (Al)	May 11, 1856 – Apr 21, 1929
Nephi	Feb 18, 1858 – 1858
Emma	Feb 27, 1860 – Oct 19, 1890

William and Elizabeth Sims Thorpe had 13 children, all born in England. They joined the Mormon Church, but family and friends did not support them so they decided to come to America. William, Elizabeth and the 7 youngest children, including 15-year-old Amelia, sailed on the ship *William Tapscott* which boarded in Liverpool. They traveled on the Captain Horton D. Haight wagon train in 1862 which left Aug 10 and arrived in Salt Lake on Oct 10. There were 650 people on the train; William was 48, Elizabeth 46 and Amelia 16.

They lost an infant, but all of the older children came to America about the same time as their parents.

William and Elizabeth set up housekeeping in Brigham City, UT, and William worked at the nearby charcoal pits. One day, 7 months after he arrived, William's workmates went in search of more fuel for the fire. William stayed to keep the fire hot. When they returned, William was gone. They found him dead the next morning, naked, with many arrows in him, a split skull in two places, and a vertical cut by a dagger on his throat. This was such a gruesome and torturous death, that it was used as one of the reasons to attack the Indians on Bear River. I found this entry in a book my mom had, *The Shoshone Frontier and the Bear River Massacre*: "May 9, 1863, Northwestern Shoshoni kill William Thorpe in Box Elder Canyon."

He is listed as buried in the Brigham City cemetery.

Elizabeth was left alone in a strange country with seven children to support. She nursed sick people, was a midwife, and sold vegetables to feed her family. After a time, some of her sons got land in Idaho, so she went to live near them. She died when she was 73 years old in Samaria, Idaho.

Cliff's Maternal Grandparents
Eli and Amelia Thorpe Goddard

Amelia Thorpe
1835 – Nov 6, 1921

No picture

Eli Goddard
May 31, 1846 – Apr 8, 1887

Children

William Thorpe Hughes	Dec 5, 1864 – Nov 14, 1884
Adelbert Leroy Potter	Apr 12, 1867 – Jan 2, 1929
Charlotte	Jun 12, 1869 – May 13, 1935
Martin	Jan 7, 1871 – Nov 18, 1929
Charles (Eli) (Lee)	Jun 2, 1873 – May 15, 1946
Elizabeth (Lizzie)	**Oct 17, 1875 – Feb 26, 1965**
John	1877 – July 4, 1899
Joseph	Jan 17, 1880 – Sept 8, 1916

Eli's family line goes back for generations in America to Puritan settlers in Connecticut. The first Gozzard I have found is born in 1635. The spelling of last names sometimes changes through the generations.

Eli was a long-time bachelor and a hard living man that loved adventure. Henry told of Eli playing cards with Billy the Kid in Arizona. This seems possible for the dates of Billy's short life. There is also a story that he brought some outlaws to justice while driving his stage.

Eli Goddard is buried in Sparks, Nevada, at the grounds of the Nevada Asylum. I have seen a copy of his death certificate where his cause of death was heart problems. He had been living in the Nevada Asylum for 4 years, 2 months. The birthday is the same and lists his occupation as a stagecoach driver so I am confident it is our Eli. It states on the website that since there weren't old folks' homes then that many older people

 ended up in the asylum. The graves weren't marked with headstones and in the year of his death there are no listings of burials. The graveyard was discovered when a road was being built and the machinery uncovered graves.

Amelia married young to a man named William Hughes. Nine months later they were parents of a son. This marriage soon ended in divorce. She then married Stephen Potter, had another son and got another divorce.

In October 1868, 22-year-old Amelia and Eli Goddard, 34, married in Malad. Amelia brought her two young boys to the union and they were soon parents of six more.

(Alma wrote) *Lizzie's brother, John, was killed while out in the timber getting wood. He had several arrows in him, but his family blamed it on the Mormons instead of the Indians. He, a gentile, was living with his sister. She was a Mormon, but she let a Gentile live with her. In those days you couldn't do that. That is why my grandmother Lizzie didn't like Mormons.*

This is another family story that I can't make jive with the facts. He was killed all right, but he was shot. They found him on a rocky ledge and had trouble getting to him because his dog was so protective. No reason was found for his death. Because he was tending sheep, he may have been a casualty of the sheep/cattle wars.

Of course it wasn't sanctioned by the church, but Mormon men sometimes wore Indian garb so they wouldn't be blamed for these acts. In my family tree we may have 2 of these atrocities. Isabell Goodenough Reid's sister and her husband were also killed, and Mormons were blamed by the family.

Joseph was a favorite uncle to Cliff. He was an alcoholic. He stayed for a time with Henry and Lizzie where he didn't have anything to drink, and recovered. He left for a job and they heard later he died. They thought if he hadn't left, he might still be alive.

Amelia Thorpe Goddard died at 42 when their daughter Lizzie was about thirteen. She is buried in the Samaria Cemetery but we couldn't find her stone. Her mother and lots of other Thorpes are there as well.

Eli would stay at the Stage stop in Collinston when he went through town. On one trip after Amelia had died, he asked his friends, the Jemmetts, if they would take Lizzie to raise because he thought a daughter needed more care than he could offer with his job. Harry and Eliza had a daughter Dottie about the same age and it worked out well.

Cliff's Parents
Henry and Elizabeth Goddard Jemmett

Henry Jemmett
Mar 20, 1871 - Dec 19, 1948

Elizabeth (Lizzie) Goddard Jemmett
Oct 17, 1875 - Feb 26, 1965

Children

Clifford	**July 9, 1893 – Sept 19, 1987**
Elsie	Feb 22, 1896 - Feb 13, 1990
Frank	Dec 8, 1904 – Nov 23, 1979
Walter Monroe	about 1907- about 1907
Eva	Oct 30, 1909-Oct 3, 2002
Russell	June 5, 1914 - Dec 12, 2002

Jemmett Timeline

1887- Henry comes to Cedar Creek

1887- Henry helps build the Just House

1887- Lizzie goes to live with Harry and Eliza Jemmett

    1890- Harry Jemmett is Constable in Collinston

      1892- Henry and Lizzie wed

        1893- Cliff born

1900- Henry and Lizzie buy the Cove house and property

1900- Harry and Eliza move to Shelley

1904- Harry Jemmett died

1912- Eliza Jemmett died

1948- Henry Jemmett died

1965- Lizzie Jemmett died

(Russell wrote) *It must have been quite a wagon train when Bill Jemmett and his new bride left Utah. Bill had been told of the wonderful country around John Day Lake which is Grays Lake now. Bill had a small bunch of cattle and horses and had dreams of being a cattle king in the part of the country he had heard so much about. Bill wasn't too much on work if he could get someone to do it for him. Everything I've been told he wasn't too much of a cowboy so he had to have someone to take care of the stock, and that's where my father came in. He was going to help him get settled. I would like to dedicate these stories to my father, Henry Jemmett, the last of the old-time cowboys. I can truthfully say he was a good one. He could ride with the best; he was also pretty good with a rope. He was a teller of tall tales but it would surprise you how many of them were true, sometimes truth is stranger than fiction.*

Dad said when they got to Grays Lake, it had been a hard winter, there wasn't any feed and there were dead horses and cattle everywhere. They went over the hills, hunting feed for the stock and when they dropped over into the Cedar Creek Country, it was a paradise. The grass was clear to the skirts of the saddle and when the wind blew it would almost make you sea-sick.

Henry found work downriver at the Just ranch. He was hired to help make bricks for their big house from a clay bank a short distance from the Blackfoot River. This is where Fred Bennett (my grandmother Agnes's oldest brother) and Henry became friends.

Henry Jemmett loved the cowboy life. At one time, he trailed cattle from Arizona to Montana Powder River Country. He worked odd jobs, but his first love was horses. Wild horses were for the taking in the Raft River area. He broke horses and was proud to say that he never had a horse he couldn't tame. (Alma wrote) *Grandpa was an accomplished "horse trader" and more or less by this means built up and lost several small fortunes to the rough demands of "life in the far west."*

Henry liked the Blackfoot River area and decided to stay. The same year he came to Idaho, Lizzie went to live with Harry and Eliza. Henry saw Lizzie grow up when he returned home to see his family periodically.

On one visit to Utah, Henry brought Lizzie along with his sister Dot to Idaho to see Emma Twitchell, their older sister. They happened to run into Al (Alma) Thorpe, Lizzie's uncle.

(Daphne wrote) *Al took it for granted that Henry was cut of the same cloth as himself and meant no good. He wanted Emma Just to go and try to persuade Lizzie to live with her. (Emma knew Henry, building the house, and knew he was honorable.) She refused. Henry Jemmett was angry, and resented the implication very much, especially as he knew so much muck about Al Thorpe. It didn't look very logical that he was concerned about his niece's morals.*

(Alma wrote in the Bingham County book) *Lizzie was now fifteen. She was charming with her sweetness and pleasing combination of ladylike manners and high spirits, but she wouldn't say yes to Henry's proposal of marriage. It was another year and Henry had about given up on thoughts of marriage when Lizzie got word to him that she had changed her mind.*

That suited him fine, but the timing was bad. Henry was then involved in the clean-up of the Wolverine horse thief operation, the Summers Gang. There were several hundred horses in the Wolverine Basin when the case blew open, someone was needed to take care of them until their rightful owners could claim them. Across the hills was Henry Jemmett with his herd cattle and he was someone the sheriff and his deputies knew and trusted. Henry was appointed the job. They were rounded up and moved over to Cedar Creek, where he could watch them. Rumors abounded that some members of the gang were still at large. It was during this time when Lizzie said yes.

Dad Summers Gang

(Alma wrote) *They brought stolen horses from Lost River, Raft River and many other places to Wolverine and kept them hidden there in the canyon. Their plan was to take them over the hills to Canada, Utah or Mexico. These crooks had a perfect "blind," a home complete with milk cows situated at the mouth of the canyon, the owner was known as "Dad Summers."*

The gang was reported to include Sam Borup, someone named Racehorse, and Al Thorpe (Lizzie's Goddard Jemmett's uncle), among others. Al was a rough character. When the gang was being arrested, Al skipped the country to Montana with an Indian woman. Later Indians moved here from Montana with the Thorpe last name.

*In the Blackfoot News dated July 11, 1892, "Judge Stevens gladdened the hearts of Henry Jemmett and Lizzie Goddard Monday evening of this week by quoting the stereotyped speech so dearly beloved and admired by young and loving hearts "I now pronounce you man and wife, and whom God hath joined together, let no man put asunder."*r

(Alma wrote) *The next day when Henry and Lizzie arrived at the little log cabin on Cedar Creek they were met with disturbing news. Someone was trying to run off the horses.*

Henry buckled on his gun belt, saddled up and galloped away, leaving Lizzie alone except for the little two-year-old brother who was left in her care. He was gone for two days. Lizzie was so frightened; she claimed it marked her for life. Henry had to ride constantly to keep the horses together.

Then a rifle bullet creased his saddle horn, and another cut a hole in his chaps. He rode out of range as fast as his horse could run, then circled back to try to get a look at his assailant. No luck. The bushwhacker must have traveled just as fast in the other direction when the shots missed their mark. Since Henry didn't know if whoever had shot at him, would try again, he beat it home for help. Staying just long enough to reassure Lizzie, he rode away to find Johnny Lyon, a friend and sharpshooter from the army. From then on, until the horses were delivered, Johnny was his shadow. There was no more shooting.

Children of Henry and Lizzie Jemmett

Clifford
July 9, 1893 – Sept 19, 1987
Married Daphne Webb
Children - Lois, George, Henry, Alma, Les, Joe, Lou, Bill, Jean

Elsie
Feb 22, 1896 - Feb 13, 1990
married John Dial

John and Elsie Dial   Elsie and her daughters Thelma, Betty and Nona

Henry Jemmett liked John Dial. He took him to the Hills to work and that is where Elsie fell for him.

(Alma wrote) *John was sent to the Lockyers to get the mail. (The Lockyers had the Post Office before the Jemmetts.) He was a big boy but a Lockyer boy was lying in wait and "sucker punched" John. He went crying home. The next day Henry and John went back and with Henry coaching, soundly beat this boy.*

Aunt Elsie had a saying that we quote quite often. "There is always something, to take the joy out of life."

Children of John and Elsie

 **Thelma** married Bob Fowler

 **Nona** married Bob Pfeifer

 **Betty** (twins) married Larry Polson

 **Robbie** (twins) married Velva Beasley

Continuing Children of Henry and Lizzie Jemmett

Frank
Dec 8, 1904 – Nov 23, 1979
Buried in Owyhee

Frank and Frances

Frank had a mail-order bride, Frances Bado. .
(Alma wrote) *They had two sons and one daughter. The wife thought work was beneath the kids so they were worthless. Les tried to help the family after Frank died, the church planted the farm but the kids wouldn't irrigate the land and they lost it.* Dad said Frank had a little farm by Boise and had a herd of Scottish Highland cattle. Mom and Dad met the daughter at Les's once and thought she was pretty good, but she and Les had a falling out and they haven't seen her since.

Russell was asked about Frank. He said he had a temper and wasn't able to be close to him.

Walter Monroe
Born and died in 1907

This baby is the other Walter baby that is confusing. They both are named Walter, and are not buried with their parents. This Jemmett baby is buried in Emma and Scaley Monroe's plot. He has Monroe for his middle name but they are 7 years apart in birth. I wonder if he was given the name in honor of the baby Emma and Scaley lost.

Eva
Oct 30, 1909 - Oct 3, 2002
Married Elmer Jones

(Daphne wrote) *When Eva was born it was on the "Sand Ranch" in Upper Presto where her parents were making a trial run at valley farming while keeping the ranch in the hills.*

(Alma wrote) *Eva loved her Cove, the surrounding hills and the Blackfoot River. Her dad at that time either owned or leased most of the big flats around Cedar Creek. Just a kid, Eva had the job of cowgirl and stock overseer. So, when her home chores were finished, she would fly away on her pinto pony, checking the cattle and the sheep, making sure they were all where they belonged or move them to a new place.*

Eva was about 15 when she was living at her mother's boarding house and Elmer lived there too. He talked her into marrying him. They lived in the Teton Basin for a while until they moved to Firth. They had lots of kids but Eva was widowed young and had to raise them alone.

Children of Eva and Elmer Jones

Joyce, Melvin Paul, Gerald Dean, Fay Elizabeth, Jewel Garland, Connie Eva, Teddy Lamar, Brent and Blaine (twins), Randy

Continuing Children of Henry and Lizzie Jemmett

Russell
June 5, 1914 - Dec 12, 2002
Married Maurene Brown (Chet Brown's sister) divorced

Russell was born in Shelley after Eliza's death. Russell was close to his nephew George's age and they were lifelong friends.

(Alma wrote) *Lois made Russell and Maurene a cute quilt that had sunbonnet ladies around one center cowboy. She (Maurene) sold the quilt and made the family sad it wasn't kept in the family. Maurene made another of the same pattern that was not nearly as good.*

Russell married Irene Ryan and had a daughter he didn't

raise. Many years later, she looked up Russell. She broke Russell's heart after she and her loser boyfriend stole his car, tools and some money. She disappeared for a long time, but they got together later and made amends.

Russel spent many years in Washington State. He worked in the lumber business loading cut logs on big trucks five or six years. He had a job as beaver control for the state of Washington. He got $7.00 for each beaver pelt and could trap anything else in season. He said he made pretty good money and worked night and day. He noted the more you make, the more you want to make. He wished he had a good partner like George and it would have been wonderful. He had that job about 5 years too.

Ever the outdoorsman, he gathered bark and ferns in the forest in his later years. The bark was used to make medicine. The ferns were used by florists in their floral arrangements.

Russell married Leona and they had about 25 years together. They both were working in Washington picking ferns when they met. This was written on Russell's funeral card:

Dearest Russell,
Our years were very precious. You were kind and very dear to me and I'll always keep you in my memories. Thanks for treating me like a queen. Your wife Leona, Ma Ma.

Leona Belcher

Russell Jemmett wrote his life story, *"The Life and Travels of the Kid Trapper."* I have used lots of things in the text of Lizzie and Henry's section, trapping with George, and his very interesting service in WWII. We are blessed that Russell wrote this.

Jim Mattson became a good friend to Russell Jemmett in his last years. When Jim would visit, Russell would come crippling out of the bedroom with his oxygen tank, "Jim, I need a new carcass." He would take his pills, have some coffee and soon his eyes would shine and he would start talking and laughing.

After Russell died, Mom had a dream that her mother Daphne was telling her there was a mix up in the graves. She thought she must have had several dreams about it one night. In the one she remembered the best, there were straw bales and something leaning against them. Mom and Dad went to the graveyard and she saw the bale image exactly as she had seen it in her dream. She realized Russell was going to be buried on a site that was reserved for her and Fred. They set the cemetery caretaker straight. Daphne died before they had purchased the two burial sites. Mom was glad to get that contact with her mom. She was looking after her interests from Heaven.

Cliff, Elsie, Eva, Frank and Russell

Lizzie and Henry Jemmett - The Early Years

When Henry and Lizzie were first married in 1892, they had a cabin in what was known as "The Swamp." It was east up Cedar Creek. Henry had a scythe and an axe when he went to the hills to homestead.

(Alma wrote) *The Indians who made the yearly trip to get game used the "Old Indian Trail." They would cross the Blackfoot River from the Reservation at the upper Cove and continue up Cedar Creek to Blue Mt. George said the marks from the travois could be seen coming down the mountain to the river. I told in my book,* Along the Rivers, *about the Indians stopping at their place on Cedar Creek to visit and giving my grandmother a shoulder of game and showing her how to smoke it.*

(Alma wrote) *Grandpa (Henry) got credit for several years from John A Shelley. Everything he could take in to sell went on the store bill. Dad (Cliff) remembers him going in for winter supplies and bringing back, among other things, 7 lbs. of Arbuckle coffee for $1.00 and 100 lbs. of sugar for $4.50. Grandpa got his mower and rake from Shelley on credit.*

(Russell wrote) *My mother has told me many times life was very simple; it kept their noses to the grindstone. Dad took a job herding sheep to get them through the first winter. Dad butchered a fat horse so they would have meat and lard. Mother ground wheat in the coffee grinder to make bread. Mother said the first wheat they grew, Dad cut with a scythe and swept the round corral out and put it in the corral and run a bunch of horses in and let them stomp the grain out. Then they poured it from one bucket to the other and let the wind blow the chaff out of it.*

When Henry bartered, he often had the other party throw in a lamb or chicken, goat etc. to the deal. That way they had a menagerie of animals that would multiply. Lizzie was in charge of them. Elsie said she would take the chicks away from the hen so she would get another set of eggs. This way she quickly got lots of chickens.

(Daphne wrote) *When Lizzie was ready to deliver her first child, Howard was taken back to Eliza and Harry. Lizzie often spoke of how small and sickly Cliff was and how neither she nor Eliza expected him to survive. Then when Eliza was called to another maternity case across the Bear River she could only look back across the expanse, unable to check on the baby, hoping the young mother could keep him alive until she could return.* Cliff surprised them both.

(Daphne wrote) *Lizzie, with her new baby Clifford, came from Collinston, Utah, to Blackfoot on the train. Henry was supposed to meet her and take her up to their home in the hills, but when she arrived no one was there. Mr. Davidson, Mary Borup's father, was a lawman in Blackfoot. He observed that she had not been met. He took her to his home where she was treated very kindly. Mrs. Davidson shared her own bed and gave the young mother excellent advice on helping the baby who had the sniffles. Henry arrived the next day.*

(Russell wrote*) Mother told me one time quite a bunch of Indians came through and camped by them on the creek. They had a little blond girl with them.* (thinking she must have been kidnapped) *Dad tried to trade them some horses for her but they wouldn't trade. They never saw her again.*

(Russell wrote) *Dad and Scaley bought some pigs, too many, and too soon they ran out of feed. They were into everything, even the garden which almost cost my mother her foot and leg. An old mother pig got out of the pasture and mother and the old dog were trying to get her back where she belonged. The old pig took after the dog and mother jumped the ditch to get away from her and landed on a charred willow stump. It broke off leaving a piece of it up in her foot. Mother was in a lot of agony with it.*

Elsie added what she had learned of the accident. It was a year after Cliff was born. Lizzie was trying to stay off of it. She would walk on her toes, or use a chair to support her bad ankle. Cliff was just old enough to pull himself up to stand by things. A hornet was against the window sill, and stung Cliff. Lizzie jumped up to comfort him. This step drove the piece of wood deeper into her foot.

Lizzie spent about a year waiting for the wound to fester and work itself out to be removed. It never did, so they made a trip to Idaho Falls. The doctor told them that it had gone too long and the foot would have to come off. Dad and mother wouldn't go for that so went to Blackfoot to get another opinion. The doctor there cut off the proud flesh. Lizzie had passed out and Henry encouraged the doctor to keep trying to find the cause. Finally, the doctor dislodged a piece of wood an inch long and about the size of a pencil.

After the doctor removed it, there was a hole clear through her foot from the ankle to her heel. The medicine put on the top of her foot would leak out the bottom. Lizzie stayed about a week with a nurse that took very good care of her. Then she went back home where it healed nicely.

The Lockyers and the Jemmetts had an ongoing feud which would smolder along for a time and then break out again. (Alma wrote) *There weren't many women, but Lizzie and Kate were jealous of whatever the other had. The post office was run by the Lockyers but that was a sore spot when they wouldn't release the mail to John Dial. Then the school board who included both the husbands, hired a teacher. She was supposed to live with the Lockyers but she wanted to live with the Jemmetts, trouble again. Water rights were taken by the Lockyers since they were above them on Cedar Creek so the Jemmetts couldn't irrigate their land in the drought.*

(Russell wrote) *My sister Elsie was born Feb 18, 1898 at Collinstion, Utah. She and my brother Clifford pretty much grew up together and some of the stories they have told me they must have had a barrel of fun. They loved to fish. Mother would fix them a lunch and some coffee and they would head for the river. In those days, the fishing was like they (only) dream about now.*

(Daphne wrote) *When Elsie was born, Lizzie bought a trusty old Singer Sewing machine. It was used to make most of the clothes for her children and a good share of the grandchildren's, and is still in good working order.*

(Russell wrote) *Mother made cheese in the summer time, and in the fall Dad always had several pigs to butcher and a beef, then mother made head cheese.*

(Russell wrote) *At that time the folks had quite a few milk cows. Mother was making butter and I think everyone had a hand in that operation. Mother would take the buggy with her eggs and butter to market at Shelley.*

(Alma wrote) *An expert horsewoman, Lizzie loved her side-saddle. Henry often worried about her and urged her to use one of the regulations, and to his mind, safer saddles. This she refused to do until her special horse Buttons ran away with her with baby Elsie in her arms. Henry took an axe and made the side-saddle unfit to use.*

(Russell wrote) *Clifford told me the story of the only time he ever saw Dad get bucked off. He said Dad was going to Blackfoot to pay his taxes. He got dressed in his best vest and coat all buttoned up, got his horse and started out. Something spooked the horse and he went to bucking right down the middle of the road. Him and Dad parted company and Dad landed on his hands and knees, busted every button off his clothes. He had to change clothes and start over. I know they laughed about that day and Dad losing all his buttons.*

Henry played the violin, Bill Jemmett played the accordion, and Emma Jemmett Twitchell Monroe called square dances. Lizzie danced and was a popular partner.

Lottie Johnson borrowed Henry's fiddle and he never got it back. One day he was in Shelley and bought the last 2 raffle tickets at a bar for a fiddle. Henry won the fiddle and looking closer, found it was his old fiddle.

(Daphne wrote) *Lizzie loved to dance, and ranch neighbors used to come from miles around, gathering at different farm houses, to do a "Dosey-Doe" and "Swing your partner." These sessions would last through the night, ending with breakfast before dispersing to their various homes. At these times Lizzie was a much sought-after partner, noted for her lightness of movement and quickness of foot. Henry often recounted that he, playing the violin, would try to increase the tempo to a speed which she could not follow. He never succeeded.*

There were sheep and cattle trailing along Cedar Creek from Utah and Nevada. The people that lived locally had to organize a grazing association to protect themselves. Cliff would have to fix fence over and over as the stock broke in or were turned in. Some of the herders seemed to think Cliff should let them turn their animals in overnight. One person said the land should never have been sold to anyone; it should have been left for public grazing. Cliff remembers 3-4 camps all sitting around on the hills around their place.

(Alma wrote) *As soon as the grass greened up, Tolmies and Enoch Hanson lambed out at Spring Creek and Miner Creek. The first lambs Cliff got were left behind on the way up because sheep herders didn't want to wait. Tolmie and Enoch would catch a ewe, feed the lamb, and give it to Dad.*

(Russell wrote) *Most of them range lambed so Elsie and Clifford would get some gunny sacks, cut a hole to put the lamb's head through and hang them on the saddle. They had a lot of fun gathering bum lambs. I've heard mother say sometimes when they came home the old saddle horse would be covered with lambs. It kept them busy feeding them morning and night.*

(Alma wrote) *Grandpa had a big corral where he would pen his sheep. They would herd them up the hollow and around on the hills on each side.*

Old man Love saw a pair of shoes that Henry had thrown away, with pretty poor soles. He said he'd give him 10 cents for the soles, he showed dad how to cut them off. Dad had picked up his ears because he knew where there were lots of them. Cliff gathered up discarded boots from sheepherder's campsites. Their boots had rubber on the bottom but cloth tops that had worn out from walking through the sage brush. The next time Love came up he had half a gunny sack full for him.

(Alma wrote) *Cliff practiced with the 22 borrowed from his dad. Coyotes were killing the chickens. The first two times he used the 10-gauge shotgun he got a coyote with each shot. Cliff got up before daylight and watched for them. He rested the gun over the pole and sure got one. The next morning, he went looking for the other one. He spotted him, aimed carefully and got him too. Most of his fur was obtained by shooting coyotes with a rifle.*

Cliff suffered a great deal growing up from wearing too short of shoes. One time he salvaged an old pair of his dad's boots he had thrown away. He soaked them in water to soften them up. They were badly run over so he nailed extra leather on to even them up. He said they felt so good wearing them, and he wasn't afraid to wear them irrigating.

Schooling

Cliff stayed with Harry and Eliza to go to school for two winters. He would sleep in the tiny loft with his uncle Edward. And walk the short distance to the Upper Presto

School by the old Tschikof house. This beautiful building no longer stands. Clifford is the 5th on the back row from the right

(Alma wrote) *The first year Cliff went to school at Shelley, he became a paper boy. Every Saturday a big bundle of "The Blade" (Chicago) and the "Ledger" would come in the mail. "The Blade" held a week's news, and the "Ledger" was a story magazine, one story ending and one continuing. It was his Uncle Howard's job, but when they came, he refused and Cliff took over. (Later he wanted to borrow some money for a show.) It was a big bundle, and Cliff could hardly carry it. Dad went around to his customers who were pretty good to him, they didn't have many nickels. Dad got 2 cents for each paper, he could go into Kearney's and peddle them. He could usually get rid of the rest at Barney's Saloon. Once a tipsy fellow bought all he had left. This was his first money-making venture.*

Cliff remembered a time the kids were playing baseball and he hit the ball that broke the schoolhouse window. Of course, he had to pay for it and he did it with the money he made selling these weekly magazines.

When Cliff was living with his grandparents going to school, there was a need for fuel. The coal wasn't delivered to Shelley due to union pressure, but was destined to Anaconda. The only place to get fuel was out on the lavas. White cedars, different from the ones in the hills, were very hard but would break. Dad's uncle Edward Jemmett spent all winter hauling cedar firewood for Grandma. Each wagon trip would take 2 days. They might have to make a road to get to the source. It would be late at night when they returned. Dad would hear the squeaking of the wagons and know they were coming. His granddad cut up the wood and he packed it in the house.

In Shelley, he had chores to do, including a stable that needed cleaned. Cliff was used to working more than his uncle Howard. When it was time to clean out the stable, Howard would sit on the manger and when remonstrated would say "Let Cliff do it. He likes to work."

Cliff was glad when the school going stints were over and he could stay in the hills. The only thing he missed was the chime clock in Harry and Eliza's house that hung above the roll-out couch where he slept.

Cliff Jemmett was 11 when my grandmother Agnes Just Reid taught him in the Cedar Creek School. She and Cliff continued as lifelong friends.

The next year Cliff was taught by a Sylva Hansen. She was hired for 3 months, but they convinced her to stay on with payment of a heifer for each of the next three months. She then left to marry a man in Montana, taking her heifers with her. She named her first son Clifford after her favorite student. He went on to become governor of the state of Montana.

The Cove and Sam Borup

Sam Borup was a red-headed Dane with a fiery temper. (Daphne wrote) *It was somewhere around 1880 that he found an abandoned log cabin in a beautiful little cove along the Blackfoot River about 25 miles from the present-day city* (of Blackfoot). *This cabin had been built by a wandering trapper by the name of Brown. Sam cleared a nice piece of meadowland, brought in a few head of stock, married a Blackfoot girl and settled down to raise a family.*

Henry and Lizzie were good friends with Sam, even though they suspected he wasn't really all that honest. He was a cattle thief, and Nels Just had lost cattle to him.

(Daphne wrote) Sam Borup had a mania for horses. He bought a valuable Clydesdale stallion which ran with his mares. As the range was open to all, the Clydesdale strain began to be seen in colts running with mares that did not show the Borup brand. It is probable that, considering the parent angle, he had little difficulty persuading himself that he had rightful claim to them. Legend has it that he drove any Clydesdale colt he found into a corral built in a secluded spot, slapped his brand on them and kept them in the box canyon until they had forgotten their mother. Then he would turn them loose in the distant part of the range where they would be brought in at the fall roundup and he could claim them as his own.

(Alma wrote about the bridge on the Blackfoot River at the Cove) *Sam made the bridge with the help of his hired man, Bill Jemmett. It was a beauty. Wide enough for a wagon, and strong enough for a loaded wagon and team or a thundering herd of horses. They built a support in the middle of the river like a small unroofed log house and filled it with rocks. Each span was made of 4 very long logs then floored with planks of hewn*

logs; the whole fitted carefully. Since it was made for high water, it had ramps on each approach.

The Borup ranch was separated from the Ft Hall Reservation by the Blackfoot River. It was an ideal pasture, and when Sam had built a bridge across, it was a very handy place to turn out his milk cows and work stock. Of course it was Indian ground by rights.

One morning when the hired man was across the river getting the work horses, two Indian police grabbed him and were taking him and the horses to the agency at Ft Hall. Borup, waiting at the corral, saw what was happening and getting on his saddle horse, took his revolver and crossed the bridge, yelling and shooting in the air as he went. He was an awesome sight with his long red hair streaming in the wind and the police left in a hurry, much to his delight. When the hired man asked if he wasn't afraid he'd get into trouble, Borup just laughed.

The next time they appeared it wasn't so amusing. They came in force but no one knew they were there until they grabbed the hired man and covered his mouth to keep him from yelling. Unsuspecting, Sam walked into the trap coming to see what was keeping his man and the horses. He fought but unsuccessfully. His wife and children ran crying down to the river but dared not go across to help him….But that gave him an idea. "One of my kids is in the river! Let me get him out." Obligingly the Indians complied. Borup hurried across but as soon as he was away, he stood and laughed at them. Turning away, the Indians took the hired man to Ft Hall. Finding out that it wasn't he who had fired at the police, he was released.

Soon a white officer of the law arrested Sam. When a preliminary hearing was held, Sam was released on a heavy bond, putting the Cove land up as collateral. When it came time for his trial, nothing could persuade him to go and see the case through. He built a gate across the canyon leading to the Cove and wired it so that when it was opened a bell would ring at the house giving him plenty of time to make himself scarce. The Indians had torn out the bridge and it was almost inaccessible from the canyon and river. When a bench warrant was issued for him dead or alive he took to the hills hiding from friend and foe alike.

One night he came to Henry Jemmett. Henry went outside and then came back and told Lizzie to fix up some food. Cliff went out with his father. Sam wolfed it like an animal. His hair was matted, his eyes wild, inches of red beard gave him a maniacal look. They gave him some food to take with him and never saw him again. Finally, a completely broken man, he fled to Canada. Henry helped Mary and the kids join him there.

The Jemmett Cove – The Early Years

About 1900 Henry bought the Borup holdings at the Cove together with the stock and the 246 brand. He bought it from Steve Hunt that had posted Sam's bail. This gave him quite a lot of irrigated land, dry farm and water strung out for about two and a quarter miles. This land was in the Jemmett name for nearly fifty years.

When he acquired the Cove, Henry gave up his original "squatters rights" up Cedar Creek and turned over the house and fencing and other improvements he had made to Mayford Lockyer. In trade he received a team of horses, Maude and Babe, from Lockyer.

Cove looking over the bluff, Cliff and Davy in a wagon, Henry astride a horse, Lizzie and Elsie in a buggy

The family was "grubbing out willows" when a traveling photographer stopped by. Lizzy made the family clean up for these precious pictures.

The Cove cabin was two cabins put together. When Henry took ownership, he cut another door and window in it.

The youngest kids were all born while they were living at the Cove. Lizzie would stay in Shelley with Eliza when she was close to delivery.

(Russell wrote) *Dad and Mother decided to go into the cow business. Dad traded and worked out and whenever he could, he took his wages in young stock. Mother said they were proud of themselves, they had about twenty head of young heifers that next spring. Blackleg hit and killed them all. And that wasn't bad enough. The old milk cow went up in the swamp and ate wild parsley and died. There went the dream of their cow ranch, for that time at least.*

When they lost their old cow, Dad heard of one on Wolverine that some people had, so he and mother and the kids went to see if he couldn't trade for it some way. There was an apple tree just covered with big, red apples and they wouldn't give the kids one. Going home they were crying for an apple. Dad made a pledge that never again would a kid cry for an apple. He started gathering trees of all kinds, he even got some from Utah and berries of all kinds, there was a salesman that came through selling trees and he ordered some from him. Mother said when they went to get them there was a whole buggy load.

There wasn't a water system, so Henry dug basins around each plant and it was Cliff's job the whole summer to carry water from the creek and pour it in the basins. The following year Henry built a ditch to carry water from nearby Cedar Creek to the trees.

Lizzie about 30 by the apple tree Mary Borup planted, Elsie, Cliff, Henry and Davy Banks

Cliff and his dad cleared more brush from the river bottom and planted sugar beets. They enlarged the ditch Borup had dug from the Blackfoot River to water the crops. "That was a job," Cliff laughed. "Old Sam had dug the ditch like a gopher. He'd go along until he came to a boulder, then tunnel beneath it and put blocks of wood in to hold it up. When the wood rotted and the rock fell down, we had to break them up in order to get the water through."

They grew record crops in the Cove, hauling the sugar beets out on the narrow road that ran beside Cedar Creek. "It was the only way in and out of the place," Cliff said. "It was a helluva road. All you dared go down with was a wagon. It would tear a buggy into bits."

While visiting his grandmother in Shelley, Cliff chanced one day upon an elderly, crippled man named Davy Banks who was being harassed by a group of boys. "He was an old army soldier who had fought in the Civil War. When I first saw him a bunch of boys was tormenting him and stealing from his garden"

Although only 11 at the time, Cliff was so incensed by the meanness of the boys that he immediately, without giving a thought to how his parents would react, invited the old man home with him.

"I was the culprit that did it," he said gleefully. "I told him I had a dandy place up in the hills where he could grow the best dang garden in the county. I had it all set up, didn't even think of telling my mom and dad."

The reaction of Banks to the invitation was instantaneous, Cliff said. "He had his trunk packed and was ready to travel before I thought I'd better tell my folks." His parents were a little perturbed, Cliff said, but accepted the old man after hearing his story. "It was the best thing I'd ever done. He sure grew a dandy garden. He knew all the answers." Cliff said.

During the Civil War, Davy was sitting down and was shot by a sniper in the knee and was left somewhat crippled. Another accident later made him stooped. He was hitching a team when one horse got away. Davy jumped on the other horse, but didn't put up the tugs when he mounted. The horse caught his leg in the tugs, fell and pinned Davy, neither able to move. Sam Borup and his partner happened to find him. They were sure he was dead, but Davy recovered though forever after was very stooped.

With the help of Banks's green thumb, Cliff said, the whole place thrived. The apple, peach, apricot, prune, plums, pie cherry, raspberry and strawberry plants produced in abundance. The fruit was hauled as far away as Rexburg.

(Alma wrote) *Davy became one of the family. When he first came Johnny Lyon was still with them most of the time. They fought on opposite sides in the Civil War so they fought it all over again. Then Johnny had to go to the army hospital, but Davy stayed on, loving the kids and they loving him in return. Cliff said he was very well-educated and taught him more than he learned in school. When Davy realized Cliff didn't know his multiplication tables he was disgusted and taught him. He had many stories to tell of his life in the army and when he was a youngster in the South and of his later life as a freighter.*

(Alma wrote) *Someone came by and needed a night feed of hay for his team. He gave grandpa a big double trap with a missing trigger. Dad whittled one out of some hardwood and set the trap under the bushes at the mouth of Cedar Creek. He checked it several days and finally heard a fuss there and came upon a Tom bob cat. He was scared, just had that little 22 shot. He beat it back for Davy. Davy told him what it was and said to aim just above the eyes, right in the middle. He did, the bobcat keeled over. That was the 1st thing dad trapped. The bobcat chewed up his trigger though. The bobcat hide brought a dollar. Grandpa got a few more traps and when he made enough money he got a dozen traps.*

Elsie told of a time she, Cliff and old Davy went chokecherry picking. They tied a rope to the top of the tree, so they could pick the cherries, Davy was pulling the top over with the rope dallied to his horse. The cinch broke and threw Davy and the saddle off into the brush. Old Davy got right back up there and got after them again.

He lived with them for several years, and was a great asset to the orchard and garden area. He spent his last years in the Veteran's home in Boise.

(Lois wrote) *Anyone who saw the Cove in its better years would never forget it, nor ever cease to marvel at the almost Paradise air about the place. Some combination of the mountains, the river, the little valley, and the seasons of those years seemed to have lengthened the growing season. Everything grew luxuriantly—even peaches ripened perfectly.*

Lizzie also became famous all over the area for her culinary ability and many riders went out of their way to stop and sample her cooking. They were also loud in their praise of the beautiful flowers, excellent vegetables and delicious fruit to be found at the Cove.

When the Sages and Justs went to the Hills to have a picnic, the Sage man gave Cliff Jemmett $2.00 to find him a good fishing hole.

(Russell wrote) *Nobody ever stopped at the ranch without eating and there was always an extra bedroll if they decided to stay the night. Everybody was always welcome. Work was scarce in them days. If Dad went to town and saw someone who was being mistreated or down on his luck, he would fetch them home with him. They had a place to stay and their tobacco and somewhere to call home and they would help around the ranch.*

(Blackfoot News interview) *The ranch was also home to rattlesnakes and scorpions which ventured out on hot days from the nearby lava cliffs. The scorpions were killed on sight. But the family tried to live with the rattle snakes. "They didn't hurt anybody and we let them alone after I killed a big one, one day and found six or seven gophers inside him."* Cliff said.

Indians came to have Cliff show them some good fishing spots and get bait for them. They never brought any boys his age to play.

(Russell wrote) *Dad and Mother had a lot of good friends among the Indians. Whenever some would stop, mother always fed them and they really loved mother's cooking. Towards fall when the berries were ripe and the rock chucks were fat, the Indians would come and camp. The squaws would pick berries and the men would hunt rock chucks down along the rocks. The folks would trade them vegetables, they liked carrots; they never could raise enough to go around.*

The following are the Indians the Jemmetts knew best:

Oliver Teton was an Indian married to Susie Thorpe. He would come to the Cove with one arrow to hunt rock chucks. It was a short piece of rosewood with a sharp piece of steel on one end. He would sit and watch where he saw any chucks. He'd have his horse and tepee in the orchard all summer. Lizzie could never get Susie to speak to her.

(Daphne wrote) *One day Lizzie was canning peas. She had plenty to fill her canner so took the rest down and asked Susie if she wanted them. Her moon face lit up like a lantern. It simply glowed. The sound was a sort of a grunt, but she knew it meant both Yes and Thank you. She went back to the house so she wouldn't be embarrassed. That fall, when Oliver brought the gloves to pay for the hides, she had beaded one pair beautifully for Lizzie. Lizzie was busy and left them wrapped. Oliver hemmed and hawed and looked downhearted. Finally, he said "Squaw say tryum on." Lizzie was delighted with the gloves and made quite a fuss over them. They fit perfectly and Oliver left beaming. I'll never forget her face when she saw the peas. So happy.*

Horney worked for Henry Jemmett. He was a large, stocky but good-looking Indian who had been taken captive by the Shoshones or Bannocks when he was just a child. Horney was one of the best hired men Henry ever had.

He was married to **Annie,** a small, erect, fine-featured and charming Indian. They would put a teepee up in the Cove, and while Horney helped in the hay, Annie would help Lizzie in the kitchen with the fruit harvest. One time when they came to the Cove she was leading a white horse. She handed Henry the reins. She said, "your horse" with a wide smile. Henry said "that's not my horse," but she insisted. Old Horney said she was giving the horse as a gift. Henry accepted it and it was a wonderful horse. He kept it for as long as he remembered.

Annie showed Cliff how to tan and smoke a hide, looking all day to find just the right shape of rock to scrape the excess flesh from the hide. She made moccasins and gloves, for each hide the Jemmetts offered they would be given a pair of gloves. She crafted a full beaded pair of moccasins for Frank when he was a baby, and a tiny pair for Elsie's doll. Daphne found one of the tiny doll moccasins at the Cove and a beaded belt which she repaired and they are now exhibited in the Bingham County Museum. Annie had lost several babies and had slashed her arms to ease her sorrow. She had a weakness for gambling. Horney would complain, "no flour, no shirt, alla time gambling." She had TB and wasted away. Lizzie called her one of the best friends she ever had.

Coolie had also been captured and was a brother to Horney. He was the chief of the Indians on the reservation at that time. When they went on their hunting parties, Coolie would lead the women while the rest of the men went through the hills to get game. They would always stop at the Jemmetts to get potatoes and carrots or whatever was on at that time of year. Coolie insisted on digging the potatoes, but would dig right through the middle of the plant. He wanted every sliver that was cut up, never discarded any damaged ones.

Coolie's squaw had one damaged eye and was very homely. (Daphne wrote) *Old Coolie was chief when they came on many of the hunts and one time he had a young squaw with him instead of the usual old squaw. When Grandpa (Henry) asked him how come. He was very proud, and said "old squaw no good.... young squaw GOOD." But the next trip they saw him and the old squaw was back. Grandpa again asked how come. Coolie said, "Young squaw no good, Alla time fight. Old squaw GOOD, she no fight. Young squaw, Mean! All time fight. Old squaw she good."*

Cliff and Frank

(Russell wrote) *There was a few years between us (Frank, Eva and Russell) but we pretty much grew up together in the Cove, it was just a world of our own.*

There were only two things we had to worry about, Dad's old Billy goat and mother's old gander. The old Billy goat really put the fear of God in us. He liked tobacco, if you had some to give him he would go off and leave you alone. In the early days, they always kept a Billy goat around the livery stables, they say it kept the horses from getting sick. I can remember being treed in the wagon many times. Mother's old gander was really mean. He got my brother down in the irrigation ditch. Mother had to come to his rescue with the shovel. It's a wonder we didn't have roasted goose. Mother had quite a few geese and we knew where all the nests were. Us kids had the job gathering the eggs and mother would hatch them in the incubator. Beings Frank was a little smarter than me, he would pace the old goose off the nest and it was my job to get the eggs which resulted in me getting the hell flapped out of me, but it was all in a day's work.

Mother also had a lot of old setting hens we had to check every morning as the old king snakes would get in the nests and stay there until they ate all the eggs.

(Russell wrote) *We used to look forward to the holidays. We kids would gather the little red seed pods on the rose bushes and along with some popcorn we would make some decorations for the Christmas tree. It was always a time when all the folks would get together for a real feast. Mother always had her plum pudding and dad always found some whiskey to go in the sauce to pour over it which made it so good. At Christmas, we always hung our stockings so old Santa Clause could find them. I don't know how they done it but there was always some candy and an orange or apple. We never got too many presents but we didn't care if we got some of mother's plum pudding.*

(Russell wrote) *One Christmas Dad gave me a lariat rope and I was roping everything on the ranch. The Chinook wind had been blowing and everything was a sea of mud. A couple of pigs had got loose and was out by the porch. I had a loop built in my rope. Dad came out and he said throw it on him. I caught him around the belly and he took off with me hanging on. Well, he dragged me through the mud until I let go. About that time mother caught up and I don't know who caught the most hell me or Dad, but she gave us hell every time she thought about it. I didn't see my rope for some time after that.*

I can only remember one time that Dad gave me a tanning and I really had that coming. Dad was always a joking; he took my hat I was really proud of and set it in a fresh pile of cow manure. I picked up a green apple; he dared me to throw it. I let drive and Lord have mercy I hit him in the eye. I felt bad but not half as bad as I felt after he got done wearing an apple limb out on me. He really had a black eye and I felt bad about it.

(Russell wrote) *One time Mother had been ironing clothes and left the old sad iron on the table. The kids got to fussing and dad got up and was trying to find a match to get a light going. He knocked the old sad iron off and it came down point first and just splattered his big toe all over the floor. He wore a rubber boot the rest of the winter.*

Cliff would stay in the hills taking care of the stock while his parents moved into the valley so the younger children could go to school.

Cliff and Henry were ranchers until Cliff was a teen. After that they started dry farming.

My family grew up many miles downriver, but always knew the Cove in our family history. One time when we were trailing the cattle to the hills, two bulls were fighting and I happened to be watching as one pushed the other until he disappeared over the cliff into the Cove.

I rode over and looked down and watched as the bull got up and staggered away. We went down and took a picture of the place. Dad stood above and dangled a lariat to where Kittie and I are standing. It was at least 20 feet.

It is amazing the bull lived, let alone recovered completely. He spent the summer in the Cove with the owner's cattle and we retrieved him in the fall.

Henry and Lizzie's Last Years

Henry and Lizzie split up in their later years. The isolation of the Cove took a toll on Lizzie. She had a rooming house in Shelley; Eva lived with her. After the Shelley house, Lizzie got one in Blackfoot, then Idaho Falls. (Les wrote) *Grandma Jemmett ran the Rex Hotel in Idaho Falls.*

Henry wanted to get back together but said she would have to "behave." They remained friends but never as man and wife. One time Henry and Lizzie were going to get re-married. She was wearing a hat that Henry teased her about. She got mad and called off the wedding. (Russell wrote) *I never saw two people who thought so much of one another and couldn't get along for five minutes.*

(Alma wrote) *When Henry moved to Mud Lake, Clifford and John Dial were partners and always good friends both cheerful, optimistic fellows*

The census has Henry living in Shelley in 1920, and by 1930 he is in Mud Lake.

When the land was lost in the Blackfoot hills, Henry bought or traded for land to homestead in Mud Lake. (Russell wrote) *Somehow Dad got hold of the Lufkin homestead at Mud Lake. The lake had flooded it; it had to be diked out of the lake. Henry, Frank and Russell went there and worked hard to prove up on it.*

Me and Dad took a couple of teams and worked around and took our wages in hay. We had to wait for the water to go down so we could start work on the dike and get the homestead out of the lake bottom. We worked all fall till it froze up. We thought we had it, but it washed out the next spring and we had it all to do over, but we held it that time.

Money was scarce, dollars looked as big as a wagon wheel. The lake bottom was alive with skunks that fall. I started trapping and caught enough rats and skunks for a winter grub stake. It really gave me the trapping fever and I have never been able to get over it. Dad was trading horses and managed to trade for some poles and posts. We got the homestead fenced and a corral and barn built.

Dad traded for a ten by twelve-foot shack. You could throw a cat through it but we got the cracks plugged and a roof on it, we had all the comforts of home. It was a lot better than the tent we started with. Now you could call them the good old days.

After Russell returned from the war, the homestead at Mud Lake was also gone. (Russell wrote) Dad had traded the homestead at Mud Lake that we had worked so hard to reclaim from the lake. It was good ground and you couldn't find a rock on it big enough to throw at a critter. The place at Melba was rocky. Dad and my brother Frank were there. Frank had gotten married. It just seemed like everything I had done, had gone down the drain.

I don't have any information of Henry after he went there. He died in Nampa, Canyon County in 1948, but is buried in the Shelley graveyard.

(George wrote) Grandfather Henry Jemmett, I remember well, for he was of the stuff that built the West. There was never a dull moment when he was around. He was an extremely ambitious man and a real mixer, at home in any crowd and a great story teller and practical joker. It was a sad day when he passed away for those of us who had listened to his yarns of the early days.

Lizzie died Feb 26, 1965, of cancer at her daughter Elsie's house in Firth. Daphne wrote her life sketch which was given by Les at the funeral.

When Lizzy was living in town Frank would pick her up and take her to the hills to visit.

Daphne Webb Jemmett Family Tree

                                                                     Great Grandparents
                                                                     James Henry Webb

                         Grandparents
                         Edward Milo Webb

                                                                      Hannah Griswold

Father
Francis Adelbert Webb (Delly)

                                                                      James Clark Owens

                        Caroline Amelia Owens

                                                                      Abigail Cordelia Burr

Daphne Webb

                                                                    Great Grandparents
                                                                      John Carling

                       Grandparents
                       Isaac Van Wagoner Carling

                                                                      Emeline Keaton

Mother
Martha Jane Carling

                                                                      Jonathan Browning

                       Aseneth E. Browning

                                                                     Elizabeth Stalcup

Daphne's ancestors were established in America for generations. The early Mormons generally came west to Utah first and the immigrants followed later. They were better equipped, had more funds, spoke the language, and as a whole were much better prepared financially and emotionally than the immigrants that came across the sea.

The Webbs and Griswolds came to America in the 1600's. The first Webb we have a birthdate in America is John Webb born on April 12, 1640, in Massachusetts, Daphne's 5 times great grandfather. Gideon Webb served in the French and Indian War and was granted 600 acres for his service. His son James, father of James Henry Webb, served in the Revolutionary War and was granted land for his service too. I think James Henry and Hannah lived on this land.

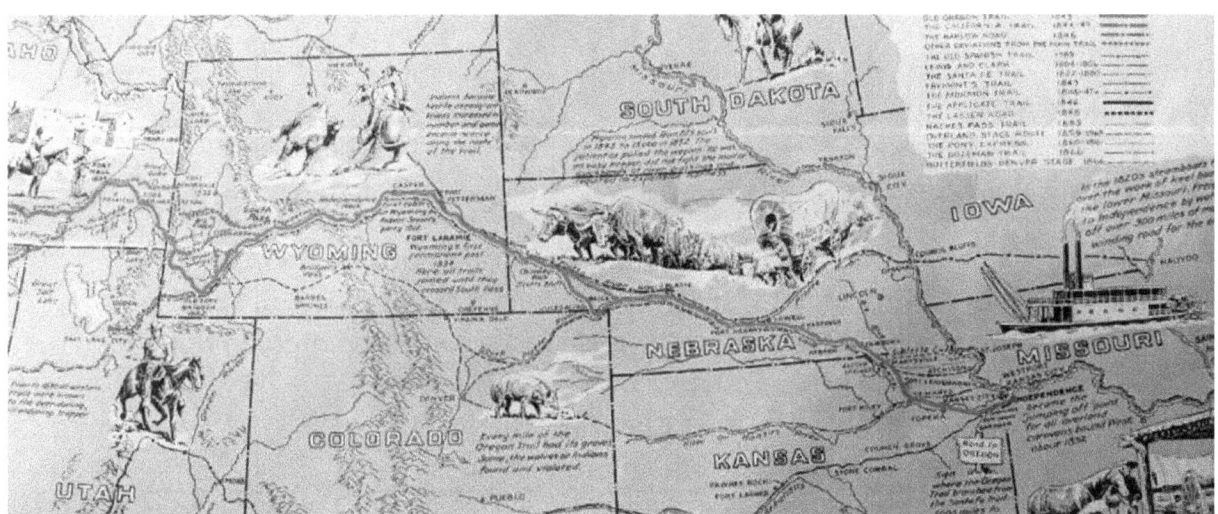

The Route West

In 2021, my sisters and I took an extensive trip from Wyoming at Martin's Cove to Nauvoo along the Mormon trail. This is the map we used and stopped at all the main landmarks and sites, like Chimney rock, for our particular family line. It was a trip we should have taken when Mom was alive. As it was, we were Donna from Maryland, and us four locals, Merle, Becky, Kittie and Wendy.

In all our Sister Retreats, Kittie is the driver, Becky arranges the lodging. Wendy uses her own credit card with each paying their share of the bills later.

Daphne's Paternal Great Grandparents
James and Hannah Griswold Webb

James Henry Webb **Hannah Griswold Webb**
Mar 21, 1777 – Mar 17, 1845   June 6, 1790 – Oct 16, 1845

We took these photos of the graves in the secluded pioneer cemetery in Nauvoo.

Children

Chauncey Griswold	Oct 24, 1811 - Apr 7, 1903
Edwin Densmore	Dec 16, 1813 – about 1893
Edward Milo	Aug 17, 1815 - Jul 31, 1852
Lorenzo Dow	May 6, 1816 - Dec 12, 1839
Pardon Knapp	Dec 26, 1818 - Jul 29, 1892
Hannah	Apr 10, 1820 - 1852
James Wesley	1822 - 1852
Elijah	1824 - 1824 or 1825
Elijah Bailey	Aug 3, 1827 - Nov 24, 1909
Amanda Melvina	Sept 12, 1829 - June 12, 1871
Mary Jane	Jun 18, 1831 - Jan 15, 1853
Sidney Rigdon	1836 - July 29, 1892

James Henry was born in 1777. He was a widower with 3 children when he met and married 21-year-old Hannah. She was the daughter of John and Hannah Peck Griswold of Hartford, Connecticut. Their first child was born in 1811 in the westernmost county in the state of New York.

When they set to work on their farm, the men would gather and work as a team to clear land while their wives came to provide meals and help where they could. A woman who lived in Chautauqua said, "It is not fashionable to be weakly." The Webbs worked for 24 years clearing their land of timber to settle a farm. There they had nine more children.

Kirkland, Ohio, home to the newly organized Mormon Church, was 50 miles west but they sent missionaries to the surrounding communities. This is how the family heard and accepted the gospel. The family was baptized in 1834, including 19-year-old Edward Milo. They left the farm they had worked so hard to create and moved to Kirkland. James and Hannah had their last 2 children there. Eventually James and Hannah went to Nauvoo, Illinois, and died there before they could travel to Utah. They rest in the old Pioneer cemetery in Nauvoo. (Chauncey Webb wrote) *"My father James Webb took great pride in his family, and he loved to tell that no Webb was a shirker, they did much more than their part rather than less.* Also, his father named all his children in his family for friends and family.

Four Webb brothers, Edwin, Chauncey, Pardon and Edward Milo, worked off and on at the Webb Blacksmith Shop in Nauvoo with their father, especially Edwin and Chauncey. It was a 60-foot stone building, attached to a wagon shop where the wagon boxes were made. There was much work to be had, but it was probably seldom that all four of them were there at the same time as they all served missions. We saw this blacksmith shop and were honored as descendants to sign a book kept for that purpose.

When the decision was made to go to Zion, Chauncey was picked to supervise the making of handcarts. The wagon Brigham Young rode in across the plains was built by Chauncey. When Brigham Young made his yearly tours of inspection of the colonies around Utah, Pardon and Chauncey would accompany him. They were specialists in blacksmithing and kept his wagons in order.

Chauncey helped rescue the people stranded in the Martin and Willie handcart companies on their journey west. A *Deseret News* item of Dec 5, 1856 stated, *Much credit is due Brother Webb for his lengthy and energetic service in aid of belated emigrants where he encountered cold storms, severe toil and rough fare for a period of fifty-five days and that too, so soon after his return from a foreign mission, most certainly he has manifested his faith by his works.*

Chauncey's daughter was Ann Eliza Webb, the 27th wife of Brigham Young. She was 24, a divorcee with 2 children and Brigham was 67. She filed for divorce in 1873 and caused much attention. Ann Eliza Young subsequently traveled the United States and spoke out against polygamy.

Mary Jane, Chauncey's sister, was a musician. One night she performed at the Social Hall in Salt Lake City, and the next morning her husband found her dead, sitting up in bed. They had been married only a few months. Mary Jane came across the Plains with Edward Milo and his family.

Daphne's Great Grandparents
James and Abigail Cordelia Burr Owens

No picture

James Clark Owens
July 7, 1797 – Jan 11, 1847

Abigail Cordelia Burr Owens
Nov 22, 1799 – Nov 17, 1861

Children

Cordelia Rebecca	1817 - 1832
Horace Burr	Jun 23, 1819 - Jun 20, 1897
Caroline Amelia	Jun 6, 1821 - Sept 1, 1895
Levi Benjamin	1823 - 1830
Charles Owens	Jan 2. 1826 - Sept 1826
Julia Minerva	Oct 17, 1828 - Sept 18, 1873
John Owens	1830 - 1833
James Clark	Jul 7,1832 - Feb 1, 1901

James Clark Owens was born in New York State and his lineage goes back before the Revolutionary War. He was left an orphan, his mother died in 1800 and his father in 1802. It isn't known where he spent the rest of his childhood, probably with one of the older children.

Abigail was the first daughter of parents Horace and Concurrence Burr, both from prominent Connecticut families.

James and Abigail married in 1816. The family was living in Portage, Ohio, when they joined the Mormon Church in 1831. Abigail's parents disowned her at this time.

James and Abigail moved their family to Independence and started building a brick home. His home had barely been completed and the scaffolding was still up. One night a mob came to destroy the printing press next door. His daughter Caroline remembered climbing the scaffolding and watching the destruction below.

James and his family retreated with the other Mormons as they were pushed further west. Each move they built homes only to have to abandon them when they were forced to leave.

James was a large man, but he moved and spoke briskly. He was known to swear occasionally. He was certainly a man of conviction with the courage to hold fast to his beliefs.

James left his family at Mt Pisgah, north of Council Bluffs, and went elsewhere to work.

As he was returning home, he got lost in a snow storm in Decatur County on the Iowa/Missouri border. He wandered half frozen for about 15 days before he was found by men out in the woods. They gave him coffee but he couldn't eat. He told them his name and who his family was before he died. One of the men went to tell the family in Council Bluffs. Abigail paid the man to go get his body but he couldn't find where he had been buried. There has been lingering suspicion that the enemies of the restoration of the LDS church had caught up with James at last.

Abigail went on to Utah with her sons in the Benjamin Gardner Company wagon train. 241 individuals and 45 wagons were in the company when it began its journey from the outfitting post at Janesville, Iowa (present day Council Bluffs). They are listed as Abigail 52, sons James Clark Jr. 19 and Horace Sr. 33, Horace's wife Sally Ann 23 and their two children, Horace Jr. 4 and Silas 2. They left in June 1852 and arrived in Salt Lake on the 22nd of Sept. Abigail lived in Fillmore with her youngest son until her death in 1861. She is buried in Fillmore.

(Edward Milo Webb Jr wrote) *Grandmother was the mother of eight children. Two of the children died of exposure while fleeing from the mob during the Missouri driving. One of the boys was killed by falling under a sled and another one was scalded to death by a kettle of boiling water tipping over on him. Two of the children who survived her lost their husbands while crossing the plains during the exodus coming to the valley, both being left widows with families of small children. Grandmother died in Fillmore being worn out with the cares and burdens of life. But through all her troubles she was never heard to complain against the providence of God, cheerfully enduring all for the gospel's sake. Grandmother possessed the gift of faith and healing to a remarkable extent and her influence of good was felt by all with whom she came in contact. Surely a life of this type brings a testimony to us of her descendants who have not had such trials to bear. Grandmother was small and of a pleasant disposition and was a woman of great faith and integrity.*

(Francis Adelbert Webb (Delly) wrote) *Grandmother was a Latter-day Saint through and through. When she was convinced that a thing was right, she did it, regardless of the consequences.*

Daphne's Paternal Grandparents
Edward Milo and Caroline Amelia Owens Webb

Edward Milo Webb
Aug 17, 1815 – July 31, 1852

Caroline Amelia Owens Webb
June 6, 1821 – Sept 1, 1895

Children

Cordelia Amanda	Oct 2, 1841 - 10 Jun 10, 1908
Marcellus Horace	May 5, 1843 - Feb 5, 1919
Estelvin (M)	about 1845 - about 1845
Estavin (F)	about 1845 - about 1845
Edward Milo	Mar 8, 1847 - Sept 11, 1921
Caroline Amelia	Jul 5, 1849 - Dec 1922
Francis Adelbert (Delly)	Mar 20, 1853 - Jul 24, 1938

Caroline was 10 when her parents joined the Mormon Church. As she grew and lived in many Mormon settlements in the early years of the Saints' persecution, she was witness to homes being destroyed, people beaten and tar and feathered.

Beautiful Caroline was living in Quincy with her family when Milo saw her dancing on a large sawed-off tree stump. Lorenzo was with his brother Edward when they saw Caroline for the first time. They both fell madly in love, but she chose Edward. Lorenzo died the same month Edward and Caroline were married.

Joseph Smith performed the wedding ceremony and later Brigham Young sealed the marriage in the Nauvoo Temple. She was left alone much of the time as Edward had to serve missions in the states. He was a convincing speaker, had a lovely singing voice and baptized many for his faith.

His son Edward Milo Jr. testified that on one occasion he had conducted a meeting where the members of the congregation were of different nationalities, but everyone understood everything as if it was said in their own language.

On April 17, 1843 Joseph Smith had the following entry in his history…. *Elder Edward Milo Webb writes that he has been laboring with success in several counties in Michigan.*

They left Nauvoo in 1848 and made their way to Missouri to make some money before the trip across the Plains. They lived there for 4 years and had 2 more children.

Edward Milo, Caroline and their 4 children, sister Mary Jane and hired man James Hoofer, were on the last wagon train to leave Council Bluffs for Utah in 1852 under Captain Uriah Curtis. They had two wagons, one driven by Edward, the other by a hired man. Cholera raced through the wagon train.

Edward was administering to a woman that was sick; she got better but he caught the disease and died the same night. (Cholera can kill within hours.) He was buried the next day along the Platte River.

To add to their misery, the hired man fled when Edward Milo died, so Caroline drove one wagon and her nine-year-old son the other. Five-year-old son Eddie drove the 23 head of sheep.

(Caroline wrote in a letter to her son Delly many years later) *When you were born, I dreamed that your father came to me and said that you would prove a comfort to me and when your father died that spirit whispered that you would be a boy and that you, together with Eddie, would be a great blessing to me.*

Delly was born in Utah 7 months and 17 days after his father died on the Plains. He was their 5th living child. He and his brother Edward were particularly close. His first memory was when he was about three taking a lunch box to his uncle James Owen when he was building the first meeting house in Fillmore. He claimed he helped build it.

Delly had to work very young as his mother was a widow. One of the first jobs he had was herding cattle. When he proudly presented some pink calico, he bought with his pay, he explained it was for her a dress and himself a shirt.

He had only about ten weeks of schooling but was an avid reader in his spare time and became a well-educated man. At 14, Delly was apprenticed to learn the carpenter trade for 3 years. He became very efficient and, in his lifetime, he assisted in building 27 houses of worship, among them the St George Temple where he made by hand all its beautiful windows and winding staircase.

In Utah, Caroline raised a big garden, made butter and cheese and was one of the first teachers in Fillmore. But most of all she was a seamstress, making men's suits and fine embroidery and lace. She was an artist too with a paintbrush.

Times were tough without a husband to provide a living. One day when there was no flour, she sent little Eddie to find someone that owed her money. His search was unsuccessful, but returning home he met a freighter loaded with supplies who needed a place to stay that night. Eddie hospitably invited him to stay at his home. The next morning when the freighter went on, he left a sack of flour for the family.

Another time when the family was out of flour, which happened during harvesting days, his mother sent her little children Delly and Caroline to glean in the fields for wheat which she could flail out and grind into meal. The Harvesters seeing them, purposely scattered bundles along the way for the unsuspecting children to gather. That night their abundant gleaning made enough meal to last until Caroline could get some flour.

(Delly wrote) *I never saw my mother angry but twice. One time was when two Indians came to the house and asked for something to eat. She gave them all she had, but they still weren't satisfied and one raised his bow to shoot her. It so aggravated her, that she grabbed the broom and pounded him good. The other Indian called him a squaw man for letting her do this to him. But fearing the same treatment themselves they quickly ran away. The next day the three returned and demanded a shirt to compensate the Indian for the beating mother had given him. This time Uncle Jim was there and he drove them away with threats that he would skin them alive if they ever came back. And they never did.*

In 1855 she was married as a second wife to Alexander McRae and had 2 more children. His first wife was so jealous of Caroline that Alexander asked councilors to stand guard over her house to protect her.

Caroline joined the United Order in Orderville in 1881 and signed over all her belongings: 10 acres, a yolk of oxen, two cows, 20 head of sheep, one wagon, a rifle, her house and lot and furniture. The total was valued at $362.00.

The museum in Fillmore has a painting of Caroline and a display of her needlework. She died in 1895 and is buried in Fillmore.

Daphne's Maternal Great Grandparents
John Witt and Emeline Keaton Carling

No picture

John Witt Carling
Sept 11, 1800 - Apr 2, 1855

Emeline Keaton Carling
Nov 1, 1806 - Jan 7, 1843

Children

Isaac Van Wagoner	Nov 30, 1831 - May 24, 1911
Sarah Frances	Sep 16, 1833 – Nov 14, 1835
Catherine Keaton	Jun 1, 1835 – Dec 14, 1915
Abraham Freer	Aug 19, 1837 – Jan 2, 1912
John Warren	Sep 5, 1843 - Nov 14, 1844

Abraham Freer
Aug 19, 1837 – Jan 2, 1912

(Daphne wrote of Abraham) *He had typhoid or some such disease in childhood which left him bald as a billiard ball. Even his eyebrows and eyelashes were missing.* (He had 4 wigs, one made from his wife's hair.) *He was a lovable, funny old man whose delight lay in making people laugh. Martha Carling Webb's son Ed said he would be riding along in his buckboard and seeing him, would wave from the front, back, the side, under a lifted leg, and raising his wig wave from underneath it. Ed loved him.*

One time at the homestead, Ed had some sickness for weeks. Uncle Abe sat up at nights tending to Ed so Martha could get some sleep.

John Witt Carling and Emeline were both born in New York as were their parents and generations before. Emeline was of Dutch and English descent. She married John Carling at 23 and had three children by the time they joined the church in 1840. They were among the saints that settled in Kirkland. John helped build the temple there. They moved with the others all the way to Nauvoo.

(Martha Carling wrote) *The Mobocrats, as they were called, went around doing all the meanness they could, to torment and they had even killed many of the members of the Church. They had destroyed many of the homes and much other property of the Mormons, and caused much suffering in many ways. But those poor persecuted Mormons knew that the Lord had restored the true church to each and others could not take the knowledge from them, so they suffered on and on.*

Emeline had a baby and got very ill. Ann Green Dutson, a widow whose husband John was lost at sea, came with her two children to nurse her. Emeline died after several months. John and Ann were later married and she raised the children as her own. Isaac was the oldest at 14. Isaac spoke of her kindness to his brother and sister.

John Carling was active in the community where he lived. He was a cabinet maker and builder. He worked on the Nauvoo Temple, helping to make the pattern of the oxen that held up the Baptismal font there. He tied up his best ox, and designed the carvings after him. He also carved the wreath around the clock in the temple or in the steeple.

Brigham Young and Jonathan Browning asked John Carling and his son Isaac to stay in Nauvoo to make and repair wagons for the Saints traveling west. Finally, after 5 years, John Witt Carling 51, wife, Ann Green Dutson, and 5 children including son Isaac 20, were able to leave Nauvoo. The man from the ferry told them to get there before the mobs had time to organize. They pushed away from shore as the mobs came screaming towards them. All their shots went wild and the Carlings and fellow passengers were safe.

On our trip to Nauvoo, I didn't find anything about John Carling.

The Carlings stayed the winter in Unionville. It was this winter that Isaac printed a small magazine called the *Union Star.* "Keep the hands busy and improve the mind." It contained poetry, pictorial writings and news.

The Carling's left for Utah with the Henry Miller Company in 1852. The Carlings are listed as John Witt 51, Ann Green Dutson Carling 49, Isaac Van Wagner 20, Abraham 14, Francis Caleb 6, Catherine 17, Joseph Mathew 5. The Brownings were also on this wagon train.

After they arrived in Utah, John was called to Provo, he was a sheriff and did many different kinds of work. He was a tinsmith, cabinet maker, music teacher, mason, judge and potter.

Then John and his son Isaac were called to work on building up the city of Fillmore. They worked on the Old State House which is still standing. John Carling served in the legislature in this building. When the railroad came to Utah, Salt Lake was more suited to be the capital.

John lived only 3 years after they arrived in Utah. He died in 1855 after developing pneumonia and is buried in Fillmore. We had a picture of a beautiful old stone but we just couldn't find it. Finally, a big stone, carved with primitive font, name and dates, and a stylized ox, was found. A descendant that knew he had carved the oxen for the Nauvoo temple honored him in this way. Maybe the original stone was damaged and had to be replaced. It wasn't my taste and felt it was very out of place in that old cemetery.

His wife Ann lived to a good age of 94. She waited on the sick and dying.

(Catherine Carling, Martha's sister wrote) *Gabriel Carling (great -great- great-great-grandfather to Daphne) was a shoe maker and did shoemaking and repairing for General George Washington and his officers and men in Revolutionary War times. When he was half soling a pair of boots for one of the officers, his tacks run out, he thought he would just use some birch wood and make some pegs to finish his work, and it proved successful.*

The Brownings in America

Daphne's maternal side were named Browning. The first Browning ancestor was born in England about 1588. Captain John Browning came to America in 1622, aboard the ship *Abigail* and established one of the first families in Virginia. It was here that the Brownings stayed for generations.

Jacob Browning served in the Revolutionary War and his son Edmund served in the war of 1812. I assume the land in Tennessee was given for service in the Military. The land was settled by *"men fresh from the battlefields of the Revolution. Few brought extensive provisions but almost without exception they carried the rifles and muskets with which they had helped to win Independence for their country."* This was a perfect place for Jonathan to grow up.

Edmund and his wife Sarah made their home in Brushy Fork in Sumner County, Tennessee. Here seven children were born, including Jonathan in 1805.

Daphne's Maternal Great Grandparents
Jonathan and Elizabeth Stalcup Browning

Jonathan Browning
Oct 22, 1805 - Jun 21, 1879

Elizabeth Stalcup Browning
Jun 22, 1803 - May 21, 1884

Children

Sarah Ann	1827 - 1901
David Elias	1829 - 1901
Barbara Jane	1830 - 1898
John Wesley	1832 - 1913
James Allen	1833 - 1902
Asenath Elizabeth	**1835 - 1899**
Martha Clarissa	1837 - 1930
Mary Melvina	1840 - 1931
Nancy Loving	1842 - 1875
Emma Eliza	1843 - 1843
Jonathan Alma	1845 - 1913
Melinda Vashti	1847 - 1926

Elizabeth was born in Tennessee. She was 18 when she planted some flax seed and made linen thread from it. Then she wove the tread into cloth and made a bedspread. She embroidered flowers on it.

Jonathan and Elizabeth had 12 children. Her husband was a Justice of the Peace and they were a well to do and respected family. Elizabeth was very cultured and industrious, loved beauty, was artistic, and had a beautiful singing voice. She was very brave when the mobs threatened them and brave living in the west.

Jonathan learned the trade of blacksmithing from a blacksmith about a mile from his home. At thirteen he saw a broken flintlock rifle at a neighbor's house. The locking mechanism was broken and other parts were missing. He offered to work for this man a week for the gun. He repaired it, then sold it back to the neighbor. He was intrigued with guns.

Jonathan saw a gun stamp of Samuel Parker, Nashville, on the best gun he had ever seen. He traveled there and convinced Mr. Parker to take him as an apprentice. He offered to do any job for this man if he would give him lessons. Within weeks the man began paying him 2 dollars a week plus room and board.

After six months Jonathan thought he had mastered the craft. He received some tools as a gift on leaving and spent all his remaining money on more. He said he reached the end of his savings and the carrying capacity of his horse at the same time. He went back to Brushy Fork and opened his own shop.

Jonathan married Elizabeth in 1826. He was barely 21 and she was two and a half years older. He settled into his own shop. His brothers and father had moved away. A younger brother, a copper by trade, said he would keep his eyes open for a fitting place for Jonathan to come.

He found a likely spot in Quincy, Illinois. So Jonathan packed his belongings, wife and 5 children and set off for the 400-mile journey to join him. Quincy was everything he could want; everything was new, buildings, plans and ambitions.

Jonathan had a cousin, Orville H Browning, who was a lawyer in Quincy. Abraham Lincoln was a friend to Orville. Since Orville's house was small, Abraham would stay the night with Jonathan. After he became president, Jonathan described their late-night talks as "two frontiersmen yarning."

As early as 1831, Jonathan Browning designed and forged by hand, his first repeating rifle. Simplicity of construction and efficiency of action were paramount in the early gun as in every Browning product since then. It brought in more orders than he could ever fill.

An Army officer in 1846 made this statement about Jonathan Browning. *A Mormon gunsmith is the inventor of an excellent repeating rifle that loads by slides instead of cylinders and is one of the neatest finished firearms I have ever seen. It was rout with scrapes of old iron, and inlaid with silver of a couple of half dollars.*

Jonathan heard from a friend about the Mormons and they took a trip to Nauvoo to investigate. In 1840 Jonathan Browning read the Book of Mormon and was convinced it was true; the family was baptized into the faith.

In 1843, Jonathan sold his shop in Quincy and moved his family to Nauvoo where he built a beautiful home and attached gun shop. (Both are reconstructed on the same foundation.) He preferred gun making, but he kept Joseph Smith's horses shod, free of charge. Becoming a member of the LDS faith put a stop to inventing new firearms. Brigham Young knew how valuable Jonathan's skills were in keeping the other Saints well-armed. He had most hours filled with cleaning and repairing guns. Jonathan helped defend the city in the Battle of Nauvoo. He converted an old steamer shaft into cannons. Using them, fewer than 300 men forced the attacking mob of over 1600 to retreat.

Jonathan was asked by Brigham Young to stay in Nauvoo to help others get ready for the trip to Utah. The pioneers needed guns to acquire meat and provide protection on their way west. Asenath started crying. Brigham Young heard her and promised that none of them would come to harm and the children would never want for bread. This promise was fulfilled.

Senath, or Sena as she was called, was young when the Saints were being persecuted in Nauvoo. Once Joseph Smith picked her up and asked, "Who's little girl is this?" She waved goodbye to Joseph and Hyrum Smith as they rode away to go to the Carthage Jail. She went with her parents to view their remains later.

On our visit to Nauvoo, my sisters and I felt like rock stars because of our influential ancestors. The woman giving the tour said that she speaks at other houses on the tour, but Jonathan Browning is her favorite.

Brigham Young asked Jonathan to go to Iowa to settle at a stopping place, Kanesville, for Saints traveling to Utah. The first seasons were horrible, hundreds died of disease, but the ones that could work, built workshops and mills. The Brownings operated another gun shop here from 1846 to 1852. If a wagon train was started too late in the season, they would stay the winter in Kanesville. In the spring, before leaving to Utah, these people would plant crops to be tended and harvested by future travelers.

On our sister trip we visited Florence, Nebraska, and went to the Mormon historical site of Winter Quarters. We found Elizabeth Stalcup Browning's ceramic matchbox in one of the displays.

The last big push for Zion was held in 1852, this was when our ancestors, the Webbs, Carlings and Brownings made their way west to Utah. In May, June and July, twenty-three separate wagon trains averaging 60 wagons each, left from the town of Kanesville. The Gentiles soon took up residence in the deserted town and renamed it Council Bluffs. The Brownings traveled to Salt Lake on the Henry W. Miller wagon train, the same train as the Carlings. The list of individuals includes Jonathan Browning 46, his wife Elizabeth 48, and 6 children including Asenath 17. There were 63 wagons carrying 229 people. They left Iowa on the 8th of July and arrived on the 10th or 20th of Sept.

Jonathan served in the legislature in Utah. He married a second and third wife while in Utah. He died in 1879 and is buried in Ogden. The graves are flat and difficult to find, but we located them - Jonathan and his three wives and daughter all in a row. We found a big standing stone with the name Browning carved on it. The graves are just behind it. After Jonathan's death, Elizabeth lived with his 3rd wife and her children until her death at the age of 81.

Jonathan and second wife Sarah Emmett had a child named John Moses Browning.

John helped his father Jonathan in the gun shop. One day he was watching his dad repair a single shot rifle, all the parts spread out before him. The junior Browning said that he could design a better rifle than that, to which Jonathan answered in a matter-of-fact way, that he knew he could, and wished he would get at it! The gun was finished and the patent filed in about a year. Jonathan lived to test fire this gun. John filed for patents on several more guns and went on to invent automatic rifles and semi-automatic machine guns used in World War I, World War II and all succeeding conflicts.

John took to gunsmithing with vigor and became known as a genius in the trade. He was respected by other gunmakers and companies, and was consulted to improve their brands too. He had the time and ambition to fulfill all the dreams of his father.

(Daphne wrote in the Alridge Chronical during WWII) *We hear from Alma that Fred is somewhat disgusted with the Browning bunch for not making the B. A. R. so it could be easier to clean. Doggone it Fred, we'd sure do something about that if we could.*

John M. Browning

Reconstructed Browning Gunsmith Shop in Nauvoo, Illinois

Daphne's Grandparents
Isaac Van Wagoner and Asenath Browning Carling

Isaac Van Wagoner Carling
Nov 30, 1831 - May 24, 1911

Asenath Browning Carling
Nov 17, 1835 - Jan 3, 1899

Children

Sarah Elizabeth	1856 - 1949
Senath Emmeline	1857 – 1924
Ann Elizabeth	1859 - 1894
Laura Malvina	1860 – 1944
Olive Charilla	1862 – 1874
Catherine Aurelia	1865 – 1957
Martha Jane	**1867 - 1952**
Phoebe Malinda	1869 – 1945
Isaac Van Wagoner Jr.	1871 – 1895
Mary Alice	1873 – 1874
Mariam Eliza	1875 – 1908
Barbara Amelia	1878 – 1928

Sarah Elizabeth
Feb 3, 1856 - Jul 16, 1949
Married to Delly's brother Edward as a third wife.

Senath Emmeline
Oct 5, 1857 - May 15, 1924

Ann Elizabeth
Apr 7, 1859 - Sep 27, 1894

Laura Malvina
Dec 30, 1860 - Aug 26, 1944

Olive Charilla
Nov 14, 1862 - Oct 2, 1874
Died of typhoid

Catherine (Kate) Aurelia
Mar 11, 1865 - Nov 1, 1957

Martha Jane
Jan 25, 1867 - Oct 3, 1952

Phoebe Malinda
Sep 16, 1869 - Mar 14, 1945

Isaac Van Wagoner Jr.
Sep 21, 1871 - Nov 8, 1895

Mary Alice
Nov 6, 1873 - Oct 12, 1874 died of pneumonia

Mariam Eliza
Mar 18, 1875 - Jan 22, 1908

Barbara Amelia
Aug 7, 1878 - Apr 11, 1928

Of the siblings that didn't die early, all were wed into Polygamy. *In 1859 in Fillmore, Isaac took a second wife, Miriam Elizabeth Hobson. She had 4 children, but died when the last tiny premature baby boy, Jesse, was 6 weeks old. Asenath was pregnant, so Isaac's stepmother Ann Dutson Carling took care of the baby until a month later when Asenath delivered her baby Phoebe. Then she nursed the two infants as twins. One time this baby, all grown up, was telling someone about his start as a 3 lb. baby. The woman asked in amazement, "Did you live?!!"*

Jesse Hobson Carling

(Daphne wrote) Once Isaac as a young boy, watched as a boat was unloading its cargo along the Hudson River. He had noticed a man untie a box that had been considerably crushed and take out a violin. The man had looked it over sorrowfully and shook his head then threw it to one side on the ground. The boy asked the man. "Don't you want it Mister?" and the man had replied that he didn't, saying that it was worthless now. Isaac then asked if he could have it. "Sonny" said the man "if it will do you one bit of good, take it. You're welcome to it". Isaac carved pieces that were damaged and soon it was good as new. He taught himself to play it and the music he could draw was beautiful to behold.

When Isaac was young, he accompanied his sister to a sewing class. He watched intently, then practiced at home. In this way he learned the art of beading and embroidery. He caught bull frogs and sold the legs to the rich for their dainty dishes. He also made clothespins by cutting a 4-inch strip of willow split down 3 inches, tacking strips of tin by cutting tin from old cans, and the tacks by burning old shoes saving the tacks around the top to keep them from splitting. When completed he sold them for 10 cents per dozen.

Isaac loved to draw. He took coal from the fireplace, and since there wasn't money for paper, drew on the hearth, then rubbed it out to draw another.

While they stayed the winter at Unionville, Aseneth went to school with young Isaac Carling. It was this winter that Isaac printed a small magazine called the Union Star "Keep the hands busy and improve the mind." It contained poetry, pictorial writings and news.

They left on the same wagon train. On the trail to Utah, the wagons would be drawn into a circle in the evening and if the weather and work would allow, dances would be held. Isaac was one of three violinists that would play. Asenath played the accordion and had a beautiful singing voice. Isaac mentioned in the diary of his trip across the plains of many dances.

Isaac told of an experience on the trail West. It seems that when a hunter would kill a buffalo, he would cut off the tail so he could prove his skill and show the doubters he needed help to get the meat back to camp. (Daphne wrote) It seems Isaac himself had shot a huge animal. Isaac took his knife and proceeded to grasp the tail preparatory to cutting it off. At just the instant he grasped it, the Buffalo which was mortally wounded in a last frenzy of rage got to its feet swiftly and with the youth still clinging to its tail, tried to charge his foe. Isaac retaining his hold on the animals' tail it turned around and around so swiftly that he was flung straining out behind him.

When they got to Utah he went to Provo and she to Ogden. They kept in touch with letters and were married 2 years later.

(Martha wrote of a conversation between herself and Asenath) *Well mother, you always loved Aunt Miriam's children just as much as you loved us, your own children, didn't you?" At this question, she smiled and said: "I have always tried to treat them the same as my own children, but I couldn't feel quite the same towards them."*

Her daughter, Martha Carling, described Asenath as a saintly woman. *"...than whom there was no purer, more devoted and faithful mother always setting good examples to her children.... I think she came as near living the "Golden Rule" as any mortal could do."*

(Martha Carling wrote) *Isaac Carling was a master workman at building, cabinet making, cooper, tuner, farmer and gardener, and shoemaker. Not merely a mediocre worker at them, but a first-class workman at each of these trades.*

Anytime there were very difficult things to do, such as repairing broken machinery, etc., they would always come to get him to do this work. He was artistically talented in painting and drawing, a talent attributed to his mother. There are sketches of the wagon train west of Chimney Rock and of Orderville. He gave lessons to anyone that requested them. He pioneered dry farming and grafted several varieties of fruit on a single tree. His vegetable and flower gardens were showplaces everywhere he lived. He even made corsages for family members.

Isaac Carling made the first spinning wheel in the Salt Lake Valley. It or another spinning wheel made by him is now housed in the Utah State Museum. There is a picture of the home they lived in at Orderville with gingerbread carvings on the eaves.

Orderville

My sisters and I took a trip to Utah stopping at graveyards on the way south to Orderville. It is in a protected valley that was so lovely. Go on a road trip to imagine our ancestors living there! We five sisters could only go in the off season so the museum was closed. We called the Daughters of the Utah Pioneers and asked if we could have someone open it for us and they were very accommodating. We were met by some shirttail relatives, a married couple that both traced Carling in their family trees. Isaac didn't sign his work but we thought probably one of the chairs at least were his. Three were in various shades of green and we were told that he made his own green paint.

There are no longer foundations of the old town like Mom saw on her trip to

Orderville. But they had a diorama made for the Bicentennial that is wonderful. It is in a soup restaurant downtown that you will want to stop by for a delicious meal.

Isaac V. Carling is pictured here. (Daphne wrote) Isaac *was an ardent supporter of the practice of polygamy, the belief that marriage in the plural state would demand more patience and forbearance, more tolerance and kindness, more industry and perseverance. He believed that the man or woman who succeeded in living the plural married life with kindness and complete fairness to all, meeting trials and overcoming them and raising the children in accordance with one another, would of itself give that person character and fitness to take their place in the highest court of heaven.*

Isaac watched with interest the LDS cooperatives that struggled to make good. The cooperative plan was favored by Joseph Smith and implemented by Brigham Young. The Orderville commune had been started a year earlier.

Everyone was supposed to work doing the jobs they most liked and were able to do. Isaac believed that except for human failings like envy, greed and unkindness it would be an ideal life. He finally asked and was granted permission to move his family to Orderville, where he thought it would be a wonderful way to raise his family. They were a great addition to the community. The children were happy and well-mannered and their parents were intelligent and skilled. Isaac with his big family had an apartment that had three small rooms.

In 1975 a one-hundredth anniversary of Orderville printed this entry about Isaac Carling. *Three covered wagons rolled slowly southward from Fillmore, Utah in 1876; destination Orderville. The wagons carried John Henry 15, Ellen Elvira 12, Lydia May 10, Jesse Hobson 7, all children of the second wife, Miriam Hobson, who passed away. The wagon carried also his first wife Asenath Browning and her children Sarah Elizabeth 20, Asenath Emmeline 18, Ann 17, Laura Melvina 16, Catherine Areli 11, Martha Jane 9, Phoebe Malinda 6, Isaac Van Wagoner 3, Mary Alice 2 (she died four years later) and Miriam Eliza 1. Barbara Amelia was born two years after they arrived. The wagons also housed other precious possessions in addition to the necessary food, clothing and bedding: a turning lathe, shop and carpenter tools, including a scroll saw, a violin and a melodeon, root stocks, flower and vegetable seeds of all kinds which the children later counted out for distribution or sale, books pictures postcards, trinkets and keepsakes. They all fitted right in upon arrival. Isaac V made looms, tin ware, spinning wheels, picture frames, jewelry, rings, tables, chairs, wash tubs and wash boards, dash churns, coffins, trunks, cupboards, household utensils, brooms, fancy newel posts and railings,*

Christmas dolls and toys. He had been a gunsmith, but now he planted orchards, gardens, vineyards, vines and flowers. He experimented with dry farming of grains and vegetables in the Cove with success. He taught classes in drawing and painting and taught plant culture. He was on the Board and in the Bishopric. He lived to be eighty years old and was buried in the Orderville cemetery. The townspeople and his descendants counseled with him and thousands today claim him as an ancestor worthy of imitation.

The men took care of the farming and stock except for the chickens which were strictly women's work. All the meals were in a community kitchen, where the women and girls took turns cooking and serving. The women were in teams where they would work in the kitchen one week, then other chores the next.

(Daphne wrote of her uncle John Carling, a son by the 2nd wife that lived in Orderville) *All clothes were made standard so they could be used by all members. John, being a tall young man, wished for a pair of pants long enough. His job was to watch over the sheep. When the lambs were docked and the tails discarded, he decided to trim the wool off them and sell it to buy himself a pair of store-bought pants. This he did and the order rebuked him sharply "Brother Carling you have committed a theft, you stole from the Order."*

As the children grew older, they married into Polygamy. They had their pick of young unmarried men of the Order, but thought that Polygamy was the most righteous. Kate and Phoebe had probably the best scenario.

Edson and Phoebe and family

Edson and Kate and family

Catharine (Kate) just older than Martha, married a young man as a first wife. Later, Phoebe, the sister just younger than Martha, was a second wife to the same man. The story goes that when Kate's husband was urged to take a second wife, he asked Kate if it would be better to have another wife she knew or a stranger. She thought it would be better to marry someone she knew, her little sister. (Alma wrote) *Martha Carling's sisters Phoebe and Kate married the same man. When he and Kate were courting, little Phoebe used to come in the room and annoy them. Then when she grew up, he married her too. They got along fine. He was a wonderful man and good father, but they always had to worry about the polygamy thing.*

I found this in the same Orderville publication about Edson Porter, their husband. Catherine had 11 children and Phoebe had 12. *They lived in the upper story of the Tannery where he worked. The annual report of 1879 summarizes: 702 pairs of shoes made, 15 pairs of boots made, 674 pairs of shoes repaired.*

(Daphne wrote) *Grandpa (Isaac) was very religious and I'm sure he thought that if he obeyed the commandments and was righteous, he would be granted visions, or at least visitations like the Prophet.*

He loved to get away from the trials of everyday life, and on Sunday after the services he would often climb the hill to where the trees made a natural grove. Here, in nearly the same atmosphere as the Prophet Joseph Smith was when he had his vision, Isaac would pray and ponder; sadly the visions were denied.

Not everyone was as committed and willing to sacrifice as Isaac. The Order struggled for about 10 more hard years after the Carlings joined. After much discussion among members and church authorities, the members had a vote. Overwhelmingly the vote was to disband; Isaac was one of three men that voted to continue. The Carlings never gave up their faith that God intended man to live in this way.

The love of the beautiful valley had so grown in Isaacs's heart that he would not leave Orderville. Isaac homesteaded a small plot using his dry farming techniques. With age, he gave that up and spent time in his shop repairing furniture or making shoes. When Martha moved back to Orderville, some of Isaac's daughters had fled south to avoid the law because of their polygamist lifestyle. Isaac was going to go too, but when his daughter May's husband died and left her in poverty, he decided to stay. May and Martha had shattered lives due to polygamy and he felt a certain amount of guilt because they were following what he believed to be God's plan.

Isaacs's health began to fade with age, but he refused to slow down. He wanted to leave this earth "worn out - not rusted out." Isaac's tolerance in others increased with his age. When he died in 1911 at 79 of a kidney problem, he was mourned by everyone.

(Daphne wrote) *He was one of life's truly "Great Souls." His motto was "Service" and he lived it to the last. Two different descriptions of Isaac. Isaac was mild and cheerful in temperament, artistic, gentle, generous and kind to all. Isaac was a stern man, insistent that his children's unquestioning obedience to the church's authority or his own. He was a man of absolute integrity and required the same in others.*

Martha

(From the Isaac Carling book) *The first 8 years of her life were spent at Fillmore, where her dearest memories are of her beloved Uncle Abe and Aunt Annie Carling and the music of the melodeon as played by her older sisters.*

When the family moved to Orderville to enter the United Order she was a slim slip of a girl with great blue eyes set wide in a serious little face, and a soft shock of windblown hair.

Her earliest memories of life there are of the children's table. At that first dinner, she remembers that a little girl who had taken her under her wing, told her that they were not allowed to leave any food on their plates, the motto being "waste not, want not." When she saw that she would be unable to eat all of the huge baked potato she had been served, she slipped it into her pocket and later buried it under a bush on the hillside.

The town was set up with a community dining area where 10-year-old Martha would have her first job of setting, serving and cleaning up the tables. She also learned to spin at this time. She was fast and no one would spin a more quality skein than her. At this age, she also made her first skirt and from that time on she made all her own clothing.

Martha loved the Order. Both as a child and when as a young girl and woman she helped in the dining room, the kitchen and in the hundred and one things necessary to an undertaking of such proportions.

Martha believed in polygamy and wanted to live as the gospel taught, so she turned down proposals from unmarried men and accepted an offer as a second wife to Delly Webb when she was 16. They were married March 21, 1883. He was 30, married and had 4 children.

Martha (far right) with some of her sisters

Daphne's Parents
Francis (Delly) Webb and Martha Carling Webb

Francis Adelbert (Delly) Webb
Mar 20, 1853 - July 24, 1938

Martha Carling Webb
Jan 25, 1867 - Oct 3, 1952

Children

Edward	1883 - 1961
James	1885 - 1887
Alice Asenath	1887 - 1889
Marcellus	1891 - 1917
Isaac	1893 - 1908
Alma (Bill)	1895 - 1974
Daphne	**1897 - 1987**
Leslie	1900 - 1920

In the Orderville centennial brochure it tells this of Delly.

Francis Adelbert Webb Joined in 1881 and left in 1886. He built houses, did carpenter work at the woolen mill and assisted in building the rock school house. He acted in plays. He married Isabella Callister and Martha Carling.

While in Orderville, Delly assembled a woolen mill with second hand machinery brought in from the east. He didn't have instructions to the machine and had never seen one before. One part was particularly difficult and he went home very discouraged. That night he prayed in earnest asking for knowledge of the assembly. During the night, he was plainly shown and the next morning it was easily put together.

Children of Francis Adelbert (Delly) and Martha Carling Webb

Edward
Dec 15, 1883 – Jan 22, 1961
Married Mary Dye

Because Martha was neglected as a second wife, her oldest child, Ed, shouldered much of the responsibilities to care for the family. He became Martha's comfort as she endured many years of poverty and moving from place to place. The only child of Martha's that Delly had anything to do with was Ed, and this only after he was old enough to work for him. Ed and Delly had a pretty good relationship and Ed thought Delly did the best he could.

Children - Van, Bob, Ed (Jack), Mike, Joff (Jonathan), Twins boy La Roy, girl La Rie.

A bad heart runs in this family as all the men died at a relatively young age.

Van, Bob, Ed Jr. (Jack), Mike, Joff

James Owen
Dec 19, 1885 – June 9, 1887
Born in Orderville, died of cholera infantum
Buried in Woodruff Arizona.

Alice Asenath
Dec 27, 1887 – Jan 13, 1889
Born and died in Orderville of scarlet fever

Marcellus
June 6, 1891 – June 16, 1917
Married Lamecia Hiatt

When Martha was about to deliver, she was very worried that she would be forced to move to Belle's house for the birth. She went for a long walk when in labor and almost waited too long and nearly lost the baby. Marcellus wasn't strong and had to be watched closely.

Martha thought the sickness that first year in their home in Firth contributed to his death. Marcellus died at about 28 of pneumonia. Martha Carling said he died of "gangrene of the lung." He was working in a mine in Utah at the time.

(Alma wrote) *Marcellus had married Lamecia, a mother of a little girl, after they were married she kept on with her free love ways and finally Marcellus kicked her out along with her child.*

Isaac
Oct 19, 1893 – June 20, 1908
Born in Snowflake, Arizona, died in Basalt at about 14

Isaac died of pneumonia. (Daphne wrote) *Aunt Maria Porter was an angel. She helped both before and after. I remember her calling for Mother to come and telling her that "He's gone Martha" and then trying to comfort her. They all appreciated the wonderful care the neighbors in Basalt provided. Ed was newly married and wasn't sick.*

Alma (Bill)
Sept 17, 1895 – Jan 18, 1974
married Coral Dean Kelsey, died 1936

No picture of Coral

Children of Bill and Coral
Duane, Helen, Bill, Doris, Dona,
Max and Shirley (not pictured)

Bill married Edith Kinney, she had children.

From the Isaac Carling book about Bill Webb's accident. *In the early 1960's a serious accident nearly cost him his life. While working in a field near the reservoir, he relaxed his vigilance for a few seconds and the tractor and the ditcher it was pulling went over a twenty-foot embankment, landing upside down on the rocks below, with him underneath.*

Somehow, he managed to get out from under, gathered up his scattered tools, placed them on a boulder, and was part way home when Duane found him. He said he was fine, but Edith and Duane insisted that he see a doctor. On examination it was found that his shoulder was so badly broken that an operation was necessary to fasten his shoulder back together.

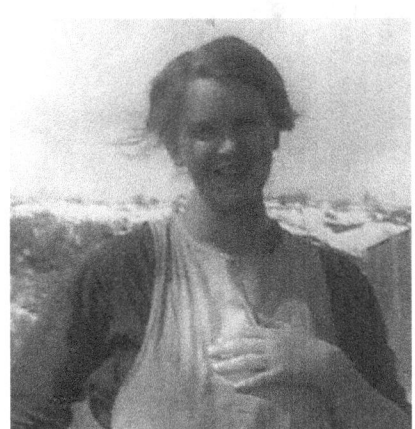

Daphne
November 5, 1897 – April 25, 1987
Married Clifford Jemmett.
Children - Lois, George, Henry, Alma, Les, Joe, Lou, Bill, Jean

Earnest Leslie
March 21, 1900 – September 30, 1920
Leslie died of an appendicitis attack at 20.

Ed, Martha, Daphne and Bill (Alma)

Delly and Martha's Marriage

It was a poor marriage; Martha was treated second rate as Delly spent more time and money on his first family. Belle, Delly's first wife, gave him permission to have another wife, but she didn't accept Martha and wouldn't let Delly provide for Martha's family, as he did for hers.

Edward was born the following year of Delly and Martha's marriage. Ed was just a little fellow when the Order was dissolved.

When Martha's second son James was a tiny baby, the family, together with the first wife and her children, and the three families of Edward Webb, started a move to Mexico to escape prosecution for polygamy. Martha's sister Sarah was the third wife of Edward, Delly's brother. Martha wrote of the comfort she felt being with her sister.

The group had reached Woodruff, Arizona, when they were forced to stop because of the illness of one of the women, and to let the horses recuperate. By the time the woman was better, and the horses rested, they had decided to stay in Arizona. They remained in this locality about ten years.

During her second year in Arizona, Martha's second son James died. She thought later he died due to a deficiency in his diet. He was a sweet child, barely learning to walk and talk. When James died, Martha was inconsolable. A young couple were traveling to St. George to the temple to get married. Delly asked them to take Martha to her folks in Orderville to ease the pain of the child's death.

Martha was pregnant with Alice at the time, and still living with her folks when she was born. She was a beautiful baby and was barely a year old when she got scarlet fever and died. Delly never saw her.

Martha had been in Orderville for 2 years until she had a chance to return to Arizona. Delly had sold the house she was supposed to live in. The pattern of her sad marriage was set, humble housing, or worse yet in a spare room in Belle's house. She would try anything to keep her little family fed.

I don't know when or where these stories took place:

Aunt Belle lived across the pasture and all the milk cows ran together. Ed would milk "Old Rodgers" as that was the cow set aside for Martha's family. Many times the cow was found dry, so it was known that Belle's children had milked her first. There was seldom milk for the older children; all was needed for the young ones.

Martha spent a couple of summers cooking for Delly and his partner at an isolated sawmill. Ed had gone to live at Belle's house to go to school. Martha had fed the men and the baby was asleep in the cradle. An Indian crept into the house and shut the door behind him. The men's axes could be heard with regularity and Martha knew he had been watching until she was alone. She recognized him as being the Apache Kid, a notorious Indian killer that was wanted dead or alive by the Army. Martha had heard of the numerous raids of murder and rape. She knew if she screamed the men would not have time to help her. Although she was terrified, she calmed herself and remembered Brigham Young's advice "feed them." He took the food and quietly shut the door behind him.

In 1895 Delly moved his families back to Utah. Enroute to Fillmore where his mother lay ill, he left Martha at Orderville where her son, Alma, was born. Delly's mother Caroline would die that year. Later he settled with his first wife in Hinkley, Millard County.

Martha's Homestead

After polygamy was outlawed, Martha could homestead her own ground since she was not a legal wife.

Martha filed on an eighty-acre plot, 3 miles from Fillmore, in her own name. (Martha wrote) *My husband and little Edward built us a one room house right over our heads. The floor was laid when we moved in, then they put up the walls and the roof. I was certainly glad to have a place to call my own and felt that it really belonged to me, because I had filed on the place myself and no one could take it from me without my consent.* Finally, she had her own place.

Through the necessary years of back breaking toil and heartbreaking frugality, Martha and her children managed to survive until she could prove up on the land. She lived in isolation in a shack that was so weather beaten it had light showing between the boards. There the wind and snow would blow through with nothing to warm them but the sagebrush Ed gathered for the fire. The water had to be hauled a mile and a half from a creek. She had to live on the land for 5 years to get the deed.

The firewood stack had disappeared unbelievably fast. Most of the food was gone and Martha was sick. 12-year-old Ed went out again, he was exhausted and discouraged, God had truly forgotten them. Then, a buggy appeared with Christmas goodies.

Delly's sisters, Cordelia and Estelle (Caroline?) heard what a terrible time Martha was having, and made a visit to see for themselves. They found the children without shoes and with only the barest necessities of life. They helped Ed gather more wood, then got in touch with Delly. He had better check on his family or he wouldn't have a family.

They later brought Alma a pair of shoes. When Martha accepted them gladly, Delly was mad. He thought this made it look like he couldn't take care of his children.

Martha had her seventh child, a daughter Daphne, November 5, 1897. Cordelia, Delly's sister, was a midwife and found a shack close to Martha, so she could be close to help with the delivery. As soon as she was able, Martha took Daphne home to the shack on the homestead.

The homestead was outside of Fillmore, 147 miles from Orderville, Utah, where Martha's father and sisters lived. When Isaac Carling came to see the baby, he started lining the house with clay and also made doors for the openings where only quilts had hung.

One winter all the chickens died but one that had made its way to the neighbors. The man wanted to give it back to Martha, but she was reluctant as it's worth was probably used up by the feed it had taken. The man said if she didn't want it, he would buy it from her for the going price. Martha received a 25-cent piece, which came in very handy.

Times were very tough at one point - no meat, no flour, no potatoes. Young Edward went to the bishop and asked for work so he could buy food. The bishop couldn't help him in this way, but when he found out their living conditions, went to the tithing store and gave Ed a side of meat and a sack of flour. Ed was so happy and proud to have helped the family.

Martha also had a son, Leslie, in 1900, when Daphne was about 3. So, while Martha was caring for her older children and they were living in such a sorry state, she had two more babies. Delly was a carpenter by trade while the family lived in a shack. And amazingly, the pregnancies continued!

Delly wanted to homestead a piece of ground next to Martha and bring his other family there. At first Martha was agreeable as she was lonely there and the boys were getting to the age when they needed a father's guidance. But after she found out Delly was going to use the sale of her homestead to buy the ground for his first wife, she drew the line.

She had suffered too much to give up her homestead. Delly told Martha "You better do as I say, or you can just leave!" She said, "that's what I will do then." She asked the authorities to arrange a separation.

Martha in retrospect thought she should have told someone in the church authorities and had the situation addressed. She thought it was the greatest sin to divorce, but after 18 years she finally did. Even though she had such a bad experience with Delly, she never wavered in her faith and wanted all her children to forgive and accept the truth of the gospel.

About this time she received word that her brothers and several of her sisters had moved to Mexico. Martha wished to join them but wasn't able to and as it turned out, years later they were forced to leave all their possessions behind and move North due to the Mexican revolution.

Isaac Sr. with Daphne on his lap, Alma, Marcellus at top, Isaac, Martha with Leslie on her lap, Edward in front

Back to Orderville

With the sale of her homestead, Martha once again settled in Orderville, buying a small house on the outskirts of the village. She eked out a living taking in washing while Ed tended sheep whenever he could get a job. Isaac Carling often lived with them to contribute as much as he could to their welfare. Her mother Aseneth had died in 1899.

(Alma wrote) *Daphne was 3 years old when they moved from the homestead back to Orderville. She had pleasant memories of life there. Her best friends and cousins, Elda and Alice, sleigh riding in the summer on the steep incline of clay banks, and a rock school where she learned her ABC's. After she moved to Idaho, she saved her pennies to take a trip back, which never happened.*

Elda, Alice and Daphne made a familiy of rag dolls by rolling up a pencil sized piece of cloth and sewing a similar but shorter piece across for the arms. The face was inked on of course, and wardrobes of all imaginable sorts fashioned by small girls as soon as they could thread a needle and work the shears.

(From the notes Lois wrote) *Daphne had a constant companion in Elda her cousin in Orderville. She loved her dearly but it was also tinged with envy. Elda would climb on grandfather Isaac's lap and cuddle up to him. It was evident they loved each other very much. Daphne was shy and when he would set her on his lap would sit there stiffly, wanting very much the love he showed Elda but probably giving the impression she'd rather get down. The two made a family of rag dolls which Daphne packed into a box and gave them tearfully to Elda, "you can have these." Elda took them and said ungraciously, "I know it."*

When Daphne and Elda were both grown, they saw each other. Elda was beautiful and thin; Daphne was expecting her first child and felt dowdy. Elda didn't seem pleased to see her. Not a very happy reunion.

(Daphne wrote) *We children were often at Aunt May's, probably because she was the sister nearest mother's age, or it could be that as she was the poorest sister, mother felt more at home with one in such circumstance.*

However, they were not nearly as poverty stricken as we were. And Auntie thought rightly that the fare we had was rather slim. She would give us thick slices of bread and butter, which we would take without too much enthusiasm. The bread part was fine and we enjoyed it, but the butter was too greasy and there was too much of it. If we got the chance we would rub as much of it off as we could, it then suited us much better.

Another favorite dish was clabber milk. Whenever we had or could obtain milk we liked to leave a pan un-skimmed and let it sour. The thick clabber with its dressing of sour cream was considered one of the greatest delicacies. "I like clabber milk worse than anything" Leslie used to sa,y and we all agreed with the thought.

Some of the people insisted on sugar being sprinkled on top of the pan but we loved it just as it was. Mush and milk for breakfast, bread and milk or clabber milk for supper. They were easy meals to prepare, and how lucky we felt when we had the makings.

Other favorite and inexpensive dishes were "lumpy-dick" or the "hasty pudding" of the pioneers, greens which included many common weeds of the area, including pig weeds or lamb's quarters, wild lettuce, dandelions, etc. and the ever popular "dutch or cottage cheese." Indeed for economy, the meals were winners, and bread and water gravy was a staple diet for a good many. That is something of which I was very fond, and even now at times I feel an urge to make a meal out of greens and gravy although I do prefer it made with milk.

(Daphne wrote of the house in Orderville) The 3-room house with the big friendly fireplace and mantle, the smooth rock hearth and the glowing flames that danced over the logs. I remember going outside to find how they got out of the chimney and was puzzled and disappointed that only one small spark emerged. Then there was the nice board fence where we children liked to try and walk along, and the low cow shed which was so handy for my bothers to sit on while resting from long walks with their stilts.

Daphne loved her grandfather Isaac who made special toys for each of the grandchildren. Her's was a small (3 foot) table, bedstead and cupboard (doll size) these were brought to Idaho when they moved in 1904. She told how she gave them to a sister-in-law, (I assume Mary) since she had no place to keep them.

Isaac taught the grandchildren music and Daphne regretted she didn't stay long enough to get the lessons.

Even small Bill could help herd cows up the canyon and deliver clothes clean from Martha's scrub board. There were weeds to pull in the corn acreage that Isaac grew.

Bill remembers Aunt Laura's grape arbor with such tasty fruit. He also remembered Grandfather Isaac who played beautiful music on his violin and the wonderful things he made on his turning lathe. Alma (Bill) wrote of sailing across a puddle on boards with his brothers; a muddy happy time. He remembered when visiting Aunt Ann and Aunt Ellen, his cousins the Chamberlains, in Kanab, where a mudslinging battle erupted with some Indian boys. They discovered a ball of mud could be thrown with a slingshot, and although neither side won, everybody had fun.

Delly never by word or deed tried to help with their living or training. As far as he was concerned this second family might have never existed. The bishop wrote to Delly asking what he could do to help the situation, Delly said he had his own family to worry about. Martha had made her own bed and she would have to lie in it.

What Martha could earn taking in washing, sewing, drying fruit on shares, etc. was their living. Yet scant their fare, and dire their need, Martha would not accept help, either from the church or from well-meaning friends or relatives, saying to all, when help was offered, that she could manage.

The Move to Idaho

After 3 years in Orderville, Edward, just 17, obtained employment with a sheep outfit receiving a princely salary of $15.00 a month. The job was in Idaho for Leonard Cox, a former neighbor from Orderville. Edward felt an obligation to help Martha and the other kids. When he left Utah to start his job with Lenord Cox, he had 25 cents in his pocket. He worked there for a year, then rented a farm. This is when he asked Martha to come. He paid the other kids to work on his farm, even small Daphne. Ed thought the younger children could work in the beets, so convinced Martha to sell her land and move the family to Idaho.

Martha informed Delly that they would be waiting at the train station in Ogden if he wanted to see them. He never showed up.

In Firth they rented a house from another man from Orderville, the Jensen's. Mrs. Jenson called her "little Daphne" and gave her two jackets, one red and one blue. (Daphne wrote) *They were hand-me-downs of course, but I loved them, especially the blue.*

The school house was a one room lumber house and stood about a half mile directly west from the place we lived in. The teacher had a room in our house. She was nice and in love with a man her mother didn't approve of. Mother furthered the romance as much as she possibly could. When the teacher returned to school after Christmas break, she brought a lot of her mother's clothes. And we were grateful. Such things as I had never seen. Of course, mother would not wear such finery until it was made over and tuned down, and then she hated it, considering it Charity.

Daphne had to walk past a line of trees, and knowing that Joseph Smith was visited by the Lord in a grove, she was fearful. She had heard a great deal about the wrath of God. She was isolated from boys and even girls who might influence her wrongly.

Martha didn't do laundry in Idaho. Ed said he and his brothers were old enough to take care of her.

Martha loved music and her children had pleasant memories of her singing.

In Idaho, Martha and her family lived on rented farms until Ed married. Then she bought a place to build on in Basalt. Her boys built her a two-room adobe house covered with ship lap. This was Martha's home until her children reached maturity.

It was the first year after the house was built that her son Isaac died. Martha always blamed the sickness on the bricks not being fully dried before they moved in. Everyone got sick but Leslie, and Daphne less so. Marcellus never fully recovered, and it was thought the sickness contributed to his death later.

(Daphne wrote) *It seems strange now with all this fuss about relief and poverty to remember that mother refused to ask for or take help when we needed it so badly. Either from the church, the county, or even any from friends or relatives. She always insisted that we could manage. It took the awful siege of pneumonia to make her agree that sometimes it is necessary to swallow your pride.*

Daphne got it first and was too sick to go to Edward and Mary's wedding dance. (Daphne wrote) *Next Isaac got sick as I got well. After he died, it seemed that the rest all got down at once. Dr Cutler called it pneumonia. Mother, Marcellus and Alma were all taken to Bishop Dye's so they could be taken care of. Leslie (the only one that escaped) and I were sent to Mary's parents in Firth.*

Almost as heartbreaking as the illness, was my sense of rejection by my father. I was only 9, too young to realize what a difficult time it must have been to him. And when he paid me scant attention, I felt completely rejected. For all the notice he paid me, I could have been no more than a particularly persistent shadow or an annoying neighbor's child. There is a story of Daphne peaking around the house at her dad making a coffin for her brother.

(Alma wrote) *Daphne always wanted to have a dad and tried one time to cuddle up to him and was rebuffed.* The very few times she had anything to do with Delly, were not good memories.

(Alma wrote) *The only time his second family saw Delly after they moved to Idaho was when first Isaac, then Marcellus, and then Leslie died. Grandma Martha wouldn't speak to him. When Isaac died, grandma was terribly sick herself with pneumonia. They had the funeral service in Will Dye's home with Martha there in bed. My grandfather (Delly) came to the funeral and this was when the following conversation took place. Ed said, "Everybody's a little crazy." Delly said, "I'm not, am I Daphne?" to which Daphne replied, "I'm not well enough acquainted with you to make a judgment."*

(Daphne wrote) *My only comfort was my brother Edward and his new wife. All the folks in Basalt were very kind. The Relief Society brought Mother a coat and Mrs. Dye made me a dress. But I needed a father badly.*

After 3 weeks the others got well enough to come home.

(Daphne wrote) *Mother paid the Relief Society back for their help by making temple aprons of the lovely green satin, embroidering the leaves in brown, they were so pretty.*

Education was very important to Martha. She regretted taking the young boys out of school to help in the spring planting and fall harvest. Even with so little school, Daphne and her brothers' grades were above average.

I accompanied mom (Alma) to see where the Basalt home was. The house is now rubble in the middle of huge poplar trees. When Daphne was a girl, one of her jobs was to carry water to the trees. We also found some home-made bricks. Alma (Bill) remembered the boys had the job of turning them so they would dry evenly. The man that now owns the ground came out to see what we were doing. He was interested to know the history of the ruins.

(Daphne wrote) *My teacher, a Mrs. O'Brian, had come to see Mother about me getting a job helping a teacher at Rexburg with her elementary class. She said she would get me a place to stay and I could pay my way to a study course of my own. However, Mother said I was too young and didn't even tell me about it until after I was married. Maybe she was right but - !!!!!! How I would have jumped at the chance.*

When Daphne and Cliff were married in 1913, Martha returned to Utah where she worked as a practical nurse for several years.

It was there Martha met and married Justin R. Porter. He was a brother of her sisters Kate and Phoebe's husband, and her sister Laura was married to a half-brother. They made their home at Porterville until his death in 1930. They had 5 years together and she finally had a loving husband.

From there Martha moved to Logan where she spent more than 10 years doing temple work and genealogy research.

After that Martha returned to the little lava rock house Ed had bought for her in Blackfoot. Cliff and Daphne lived there too when they moved to Blackfoot so Bill and Jean could go to school.

(Alma wrote) *Martha and a lady carried on a letter correspondence. When she didn't answer her last letter, Martha said sadly, "If I had just left religion out of it, we'd still be friends, she trusted me." I think this is a touching story that shows what a sweetie Grandma really was.*

In the Isaac V Carling volume one, about Martha…..*The preceding history tells the bare facts of Martha's life, but it scarcely begins to tell the story. It would take volumes to do that. It tells nothing of the struggles to raise a family without a father's help and guidance. It touches only lightly on the problems of stretching every penny until it howls for mercy and still failing to make it cover the actual needs of a hungry brood. Of never eating enough herself so that there would be more for the little ones. It does not even mention the agonizing hours at sick beds, only to lose the loved ones in the end, or of the misery of going about her daily duties with sick despair her constant companion. The sufferings and privations of her life are left mostly to the imagination.*

Many years later, Delly went to the Hills to see Daphne to try to make his peace with her. He said, "I loved Martha, it broke my heart to lose her, but it was all the fault of her foolish old father."

Daphne with Delly

Delly, Robert (Ed's son) holding Bobbie, Edward

Henry, Delly, George, Joe and Bill

Delly was bathing when he was 85 and a fire started in his home. He was badly burned and died as a result.

Clifford and Daphne Webb Jemmett
Married June 16, 1913

Clifford Jemmett
July 9, 1893 - Sept 19, 1987

Daphne Webb Jemmett
Nov 5, 1897 - April 25, 1987

Children

Lois Daphne	1915 - 2006
George Clifford	1917 - 2009
Henry Edward	1918 - 2008
Leslie Tarzan	1920 - 2012
Alma Marcella	**1921 - 2010**
Joseph Paul	1925 - 2000
Mary Lou	1930 - 1939
Jay Willard (Bill)	1936 - 1997
Eugene Russell (Jeanne)	1939 - 2025

Lois Daphne

Nov 6, 1915 - July 23, 2006

Lois married Chet Brown and had children - Phil, Evon, Rita, Clifford, Leah, and Eddie. Chet divorced Lois about 1970.

Lois went to Texas when her daughter Evon was dying of cancer. She took care of Evon's children for some years, her husband was very grateful. Then she came to Blackfoot to take care of her folks.

She went back to Oregon after they died. She remarried Chet after 19 years and cared for him until he died in 1992. Mom, Dad, Uncle Bill (with all of his electrical equipment) went to visit Lois one time in Oregon. Bill stayed there for some months.

Ed, Cliff, Phil, Chet, Lois, Evon, Rita, Leah

George Clifford
Jan 25, 1917 – Sept 15, 2009
Married Millie Anderson
Children - Tony, Marcia, Deborah, Lorna, Allan, Barbara, Cliff, Teresa.
Married Jean Kohl Johnson.
Re-married Millie. Married Sylvia Hansen Burrus.

George and Millie

Deborah, Tony and wife Mary Jo, Dave Rossi and wife Marcia, Lorna
George, Allan, Teresa, Barbara, Millie
Clifford, Toni Jo (Tony's daughter)

Henry Edward
May 17, 1918 – Mar 15, 2008
Married Lois Pratt, died
Child - Evelyn born and died on the 18th but Lois hung on until the 25th.
Henry later married Ruby Reeder.

(Alma wrote) *The first tragedy to strike our family was when Henry's wife Lois and their baby Evelyn died the first year we were in high school. Lois died of an infection after the premature birth of their baby. Lois's father was Frank Pratt, the range rider on the Reservation and he knew where they could find a big flat red rock for the headstone. Henry carved their names on it and it can be seen at the Blackfoot cemetery. Henry used his rock carving skill again for the Alridge memorial.*

After Lois and the baby died, Henry was distraught. Cliff took him to visit with Lizzie at the boarding house. She asked Henry what he intended to do. "I don't have two nickels to rub together," he said. Lizzie walked to a cupboard and brought back $200. Henry told her he didn't know how he would ever pay her back. She answered "What are grandmas for?"

Henry found love again and married Ruby Reeder. He had an accident while working as a mechanic in Blackfoot. He was changing a tire and had a screwdriver to pry at the rubber. It came loose and hit Henry in the eye. The eye was lost and he had a fake eye. Dad said he could see better out of one than most people could out of two.

Children
Ed and Wayne
Josie, Reena, Connie
Martha, Steve,
Ruby, Henry, Vonda

Leslie Tarzan
Jan 14, 1920 – April 14, 2012
Married Edna Sharpe
Children - Beverly, Gail, Karen, Donny (died young) Dorothy, Sandy, Chris

Edna

Dorothy, Chris, Beverly, Les, Edna, Karen, Gail, Sandy

Alma Marcella
Dec 21, 1921 - Sept 19, 2010
Married Fred Reid
Children - Richard, Janene, Donna, Merle, Becky, Kittie, and Wendy

Mom had an appendectomy about 6 months after she was married. Cliff offered to pay a portion of the operation since it happened so soon after they were married and he thought it was his responsibility.

It was about $200 dollars but Dad didn't let him. Dad started and ended the story with: "this shows what kind of a man Alma's dad was."

Mom had had several attacks while she was working in Ogden. She remembers going home from work sick to her stomach. She wondered why she wasn't more concerned it may be appendicitis knowing all the trouble in her family.

Wendy, Becky, Rich, Kittie, Merle
Donna, Fred, Alma, Janene

Joseph Paul
Aug 30, 1925 – Aug 30, 2000
Married Anne Nyle Wirick
Children - Judy, Joe, Jan, Jill

Judy, Jill on Ann's lap
Joe, Joe Jr., Jill

Mary Lou
Jan 5, 1930 – June 5, 1939

Died at 9 of appendicitis on the same day that baby sister Jean was born.

(Les remembered with Alma) *Our sister Mary Lou--- all I can remember is that she was a very sweet girl; very pretty, very much like Lois and you in looks, I guess more like Lois really. Blonde and pretty! I wish I could remember more.*

(Daphne wrote about Mary Lou) *Louie had had a bad time with what Dr. Cutler said might be appendicitis, and said if she got worse to bring her into the hospital. She didn't seem to get worse, but she didn't seem to get better. So when I knew I had to get to the hospital with the new baby I insisted that she go too so that she would be assured of the best care while I was gone. Both Dr. Cutler and Dr. Hatch examined her and said she should be operated on at once. I told her I had to go in the delivery room and she said, "Mamma, you know it must be a little sister." The nurse asked if she didn't like little boys. She said, "I've already got a little brother." She loved Bill. She called him her little blue boy. But she never got to see the little sister.*

Mom has some cute diary pages written by Lou.

Daphne wasn't able to go to the funeral because she was recovering from childbirth. Mom had to stay with Lou in the funeral home while Cliff made preparations for burial. Mom remembers Bill got a new outfit.

(Alma wrote) *That was a very sad time. Lois was married and in Washington then so I was the woman of the house, and I certainly wasn't much of a woman. Mom almost died that next winter and so I was a second mother to baby Jean.*

Jay Willard (Bill)
Mar 30, 1936 – April 7, 1997
Never married

Daphne had a goiter in her neck for many years. She finally had an operation because it was affecting her breathing. She stopped breathing while on the operating table and thought since she was pregnant with Bill at the time, it probably affected him. He was a whiz at electronics and early computers.

Eugene (Jeanne) Russell
June 5, 1939 – Feb 21, 2025
Married Lou Larder, divorced
Children - Beth, Lori
Married Luke Hines (Lou married Luke's wife)

Cliff and Daphne Webb Jemmett

(Alma wrote) *Harry and Eliza had settled in Shelley a few miles from Basalt. Some winters my dad lived for a while with his grandmother Jemmett so he could go to school. He also went to church with her sometimes. Eventually, due to school and church activities, these two young people who became my parents became acquainted, shared their family stories and fell in love. They both felt very deeply about their divided families and made their vows that they would never do that to their children; they would always have a family with two parents. They didn't always agree, Mom had a mind of her own, but we could see that they really loved one another. I can remember Mama saying to the younger kids, "You are so lucky to have such a good daddy!"*

Clifford had a little one-seat buggy with a black top pulled by his bay saddle horse Bally. He used it to go to ball games or dances.

(Alma wrote) *Dad sold all his winter's catch (hides), baled them and sent them off in the mail. When he got paid, he went to Shelley where his folks lived and cashed the check at the Shelley bank and got two $20 gold pieces. It was time for him to go to Blackfoot to get some courting clothes. He went to the livery stable to get his buggy and team. There was a Jewish man there who was looking for a ride to Blackfoot. He got mad at the price charged to ride the train and since dad was going anyway, he said, sure he could ride with him. The Jew was amazed at how quickly they got to Blackfoot and was impressed with his fine little team.* (I don't know if this is the team he had then, but Prince and Maude, bay horses, were Cliff's team, Prince would be used to break all the other horses to pull). *He handed Cliff 5 dollars and an extra 50 cents saying to give those good horses some grain. Dad stabled the horses and then went to the clothing store. With his 2 gold pieces he bought a hat, a suit, a dress shirt, shoes (and maybe a coat) The suit was a bit of a problem since there was none that fit. "We have a tailor, no problem. Just pick out what you like and we'll have it altered" the clerk said. The one that appealed to him had been made for a larger man. The tailor took all his measurements went to work snipping and tearing until the suit was in pieces. Cliff was* *aghast and could hardly believe that it could be put back together that afternoon. "You've got a good piece of cloth" the tailor said. "And when I get done, you'll have a better suit. It won't come apart like this one did." Cliff still had $5.00 when he got his team and started back to Shelley, resplendent in his new clothes.*

(Alma wrote) *Daphne met my dad the night of her 8th grade graduation dance. She was 14 or coming 14 (1911) and had a date with someone else. My dad was there with Mae Crofts, Daphne's best friend. Her folks had a place in the hills and so knew the Jemmett's. Mae would say whenever she didn't have a date, "My sweetheart is in the hills." He was a handsome man, Cliff at 6 ft tall, with big hands, who had his pick of the girls, but it was love at first sight for both young people. Mae introduced Daphne to Clifford.*

Daphne at the Basalt School (the pen mark must be Daphne)

At a dance in Shelley later on, Daphne saw Cliff and went to speak to him. They danced and he wanted to take her home. She was with someone else that night but she said that if he came to Basalt to a dance, she'd go home with him. So he did, but that night she also had a date. He was Clyde Bartdale. When Dad asked Mom if she would let him take her home, she said that she couldn't that night but she would from then on. She felt bad because Clyde gave her a box of candy when he got her home. He said "I thought maybe we could make a go of it, but I can see now that we can't." She tried to get him to keep it and give it to another girl, but he said "No, I got it for you, so you take it."

(Alma wrote) *After Dad became engaged to Mom they were at a dance; Mom was such a good dancer and Dad mostly watched as she was flying by with other guys. Bert Bates was there and asked Dad if he brought a partner. "Yes, my fiancé," he answered and pointed her out. They watched as she danced by (she was such a cute little dark haired, rose-cheeked gal, Dad said) and Bert said "Well you sure know how to pick 'em."*

Cliff and Daphne were married June 13, 1913. She wouldn't be 16 until the next fall, and Cliff would be 20 on July 9. They were married by Judge James Stevens, the son of the judge that married Cliff's parents 21 years before.

Daphne made her own 22-inch waist beaded muslin wedding gown. Anna Pratt Lickley, Wendy's daughter, models it here. I wish a photo had been taken with Daphne in this dress and Cliff in his new suit.

Daphne and Cliff went on their honeymoon to the Webb cattle company in Burley to see Delly. It was one of the few times Grandma had seen her dad and met her half-brothers from the first polygamist family. Daphne got breakfast for everyone, being the only woman. Cliff had a painful hangnail on a big toe during his honeymoon. Delly gave them a set of flat irons for a wedding present (4 heavy bases that you heat on the stove, when one cools down, you hook the handle on another). Cliff put them in his suitcase and had to carry them around the rest of the trip. It was agonizing to have that weight on his sore foot. Then the bridal couple stopped at Pocatello, spent a day there, ate at the Bon Ton and stayed at the Bannock Hotel. Then they caught the train to Firth and home.

They married and spent their first year with Henry in the cabin at the Cove.

(Daphne wrote about Henry, her father- in-law) *As a bride with none too much experience as a cook, especially to a group of men, he used to embarrass me especially when coffee cups were empty. He would tap his spoon against the side of his cup, his way of asking for a refill, darting glances of amusement at the others at the big table, until at last I would notice, and, face burning , would bring the huge coffee pot and more coffee all the way around. I remember how I used to feel that to ask quietly would be much kinder but he never would and the others never failed to laugh uproariously at my expense. At times like that I almost hated him.*

Then again, his hospitality was abundant, and as it was never himself that had to stand the work of the extra meals, as he never remembered to say "Thanks!" for my trouble, I used to hate to see the many friends who would drop in. They weren't my friends, but his, and took the extra work as a matter of course and invariably he would apologize for the food.

"Our cook is kinda young" he would say, "but she does her best. Do try and make out a meal." As if it would be a very hard thing to do in the circumstances. I would hang my head in mortification, though I know he meant this kindly.

Many days especially in the early part of the fishing season, it seemed to me that getting extra meals was a nightmare and my young bones would be so weary that I could hardly stand.

No, I am certain now that he just never understood how hard it was, or how embarrassed I got. Because he was really kind at heart and I am sure would never have hurt me intentionally. "Putting something over!" was legitimate fun; being hospitable was the thing to do, and I was someone new to play jokes on. A woman to do the work, he never thought any farther than that.

(Alma wrote) *The next year Cliff and Daphne moved "up in the hollow" north of Cedar Creek. This was the only homestead site available when my Dad Clifford became 21. He and his dad built our one-room house. There wasn't water where my folks lived at the time. Water had to be carried from Cedar Creek or from a spring further up or down the creek. The Cliff Jemmetts proved up on a dry farm homestead when Lois was school age.*

Early Years in Alridge

Then they moved to the junction of roads leading up Cedar creek and up the Blackfoot River. They lived there about thirty years, with the Alridge Post office in the home almost all of the time.

Alridge Post Office

When the Jemmetts got the post office, Daphne wanted the area to be called Cedar Creek. There was already a Cedar Creek Post Office in Idaho, so she had to come up with a new name. She decided Alridge for all the ridges around their home.

(Alma wrote) *We had a little 2 room frame house with a loft. The post office was a cubby-hole between the 2 rooms. It was kept locked and even some of their wanted posters were put up. My dad and the boys had quite an arsenal of weapons because of their hunting. Mom made a list once for the postal department to show what was available for defense. It was pretty impressive.*

Alma remembered the excitement of mail days when they received the latest addition of Colliers or an order from Sears Roebucks. Delivery would be on Monday and Thursday. If it was ordered on Thursday you could count on it being in the mail on Mon. If it was ordered on Monday, it may or may not be there Thursday.

The family had a generator that was wind charged. They had gas lamps.

The Jemmetts had a little phone type system between Chet and Lois's house and theirs, a long quarter mile away. They lived at the Manning house, north of the Aldridge home towards Wolverine.

Alma was a big kid when they got a radio. She remembers a tall pole with an antenna west of the house. There was a wire strung to Lois's house so they could get the same stations and one strung to the Cove. It came in the mail and had to be put together. George remembers the first words that came out of the radio, "This is KSL in Salt Lake City." Alma remembers Daphne would turn it on first thing in the morning and it was above her bed where she was sleeping. It had 4 knobs that had to be adjusted so the station came in clear. George's favorite show was the Solitary Cowboy.

They hauled drinking water from the spring which was a way away, but the water they used for washing was from the creek that was closer. If the water was muddy, they had to use the spring. The spring ran all winter.

(Alma wrote) *Dad had a few cattle and some Eastern Idaho range right. Dad Hall always took our cattle up with his on the way to the hills.*

Cliff called Daphne "Mommy."

The Jemmetts were Republicans.

Cliff Jemmett would use "somick" instead of "something." As in, "I better get somick done." Dad borrowed that expression too.

My brother Rich remembers how Cliff told stories in his later years. He would stand up and use his arms to express himself. Rich now honors Cliff by doing the same.

They had to take castor oil and fuel oil sugar for the croup.

Daphne was always cheerful. She would sing, and when her voice gave out, she would whistle.

Daphne's food specialties were chicken and dumplings and Chicken noodle soup.

The kids all wanted to please their folks so needed very little discipline.

Cliff was strict but fair. Henry remembers being bad and his dad "took me apart and put me together right." Lois doesn't remember being spanked or even scolded except once and she deserved it.

(Alma wrote) *During the Depression everyone was bad off. It wasn't just us. Dad and Uncle John raised some pigs, had a customer in Shelley. However, when they took them down, he couldn't give them the little bit he had promised, so they brought them back and we had the fun of eating them.*

(Alma wrote) *I remember shoes at $1.50 a pair, Levis at $1.50 a pair, and 22 bullets at 10 cents a box. People did a lot of trading. I mean that they traded among themselves, for a good trade was better than spending money - not many people had money.*

Alma remembers Daphne making dresses out of flour sacks. Lois had one with a matching hat.

(From Google search) *In 1939, in Kansas, wheat mill owners realized that women were using their sacks to make clothes for their children. The mills started using flowered fabric for their sacks so the kids would have pretty clothes, and the label would wash out, a gesture of pure kindness. Times were lean during the Great Depression so reusing everything possible was a way of life.*

(Alma wrote) *I always darted home at noon trying to keep up with my three brothers and older sister Lois. While we were gone the other kids ate their lunches, something which was fun for us, but which only the worst blizzard could make happen.*

(Alma wrote) *When Martha Carling came to visit, she always slept with me. The first thing she would tell me was what wonderful parents I had, both Mom and Dad. She praised to the skies, never, ever found any fault with my dad.*

Fun

Mom remembered playing ghost when big sister Lois would dress up and scare the girls by hiding in the abandoned Cove house.

Daphne loved poetry, reading it, reciting it, and writing it. All her kids liked to listen to her rendition of "Hiawatha" and other ballads like, "Who Stuffed that Owl."

Cliff's sister Elsie and her husband John Dial lived on the other side of the school, situated at the start of the Cove Canyon, and they had a claim up on the rocks above the Cove.

The Dial twins, Bob and Betty, would throw rocks across the road at each other, so mom didn't like to walk by on her way to the Cove.

Alma and cousin Nona Dial had a post office tree where they would leave notes to each other. It was a big Cottonwood between their houses, planted by great aunt Emma and her husband Bill Twitchell.

The Jemmett kids loved to go to town. They rarely went all together. When they got a car, they all got car sick.

Alma remembers seeing her 1st movie. It was in Shelley, while she was staying with her grandma Lizzie in the boarding house soon after Lou had died. Les was with her, it was mostly ads, and they got bored and left before it was over.

Alma never had cowboy boots when she was young and was amazed that riding was so much easier with them.

Alma couldn't remember having a special toy. She remembered George and Henry bought her a baby doll, with their trapping money. She was 12 and thought herself much too old for a doll. Betty Dial put the doll in the water trough.

Work

(Les remembered) *The huge herds of cattle and sheep that Stockmen and Cowboys would bring up past our place on the way to summer pastures and all the broken fences and problems with our stock.*

(Les remembered) *The many miles of irrigation ditches that we cleaned every spring. The hours and hours of irrigating that I believe all of us took turns at when we were old enough to be of help. The dams that we put in Cedar Creek to get enough water.*

They sold alfalfa and grass seed. One time they were selling alfalfa seed to Berkley Larson. They weighed the seed with their scales and Berkley thought that was too heavy and wanted to weigh it on his own scales. When his scales said it was even heavier, he then trusted the Jemmett scales as being right.

The Jemmetts sometimes sold dressed turkeys. They would pluck them right after they were killed so the feathers came out easily and they wouldn't have to put them in boiling water.

(Les remembered) *The invasion when the Mormon Crickets came up over the bluffs at the old Johnson place and all the problems they caused us.*

Alma remembers picking spuds off the ground above Wolverine. She got 5 cents a gunny sack full. They were little spuds and there were lots of rocks so when the owner saw how bad it was, he upped it to 6 cents a bag. She didn't make much money.

Alma and Les would be sent off with their lunch pails to herd turkeys or sheep. (Les wrote) *I remember Sis, about the days you and I had the job of herding turkeys. That was something! Do you remember herding them? Sometimes clear over to the Blackfoot River where there were so many grasshoppers. When we came back and got close to home—how some of the turkeys would fly off the top of the hill—above the old corrals and stables and fly clear to the house—or so it seems when I think about it.*

Mom's brothers would pick the wool off the fences; Mom and Grandma Daphne would clean it, card it and make batting for quilts.

Daphne's cousin worked for the Woolen Mills, Mom remembers him coming to her house in the Hills, he wouldn't charge Daphne more than the cost of the item.

Memories

Joe, Les, George, Henry
Alma, Daphne holding Jean, Bill, Cliff

Cliff was working in the hay. There was something hanging on his pants, and when someone asked him what it was, he looked down, "a damned little snake!" A small rattler had got his fangs stuck in the fabric of his pants and was flopping loose.

Alma remembers her dad buying meat one time at the butcher shop, probably because Uncle John was buying some and he wanted to show he could afford meat too, but he really couldn't.

Alma, George, Henry, Les

(Les remembered) Christmas Eve when I was just a little boy, at Uncle John and Aunt Elsie's home. I remember sleigh bells and someone saying, I think Mom---"Santa is here!" Then a big Santa Claus came into the room, carrying a big bag of presents. He gave me a pop-gun—boy was I plumb happy! I cannot remember anything else except kids getting toys and then Santa left and we all could hear the sleigh-bells and thought that Santa and his reindeer were sure real.

(Les wrote) I remember when Bill was sick. One night he was crying and so sick. It seems to me that Joe and I decided we'd get him to sleep so we took turns, if I remember right, trying to take care of him and finally got him to sleep. Boy, he was so sick! It was a miracle he lived.

(Les wrote) A meteor came over one night when we were all standing outside. Just about dark. A great ball of fire played up over the end of Cedar Mountain and came overhead leaving a trail of fire and falling sparks. Then the rumbling noise after it went out of sight.

(Alma wrote) The first thing I can remember, to put a date to, is my brother Joe's birth. He was born Aug 30, 1925 at Grandma Jemmett's rooming house in Shelley, the same place I had been born on Dec 21, 1921 so I was 3 and a half. There was a long stairway on the back of the building, and I was at the bottom of the steps when Grandma came after me and took me to see my baby brother. He's always been very dear to me.

Mom's brothers caught ground squirrels and turned them loose in the Manning house. They cut off their tails so they could get the bounty. They wanted to brand them but Cliff made the boys turn them loose. Cliff thought they were being cruel to them and said either kill them or turn them loose. They spent a lot of time feeding and watering them and decided it was too much work anyway. They turned them loose, but would catch tailless ground squirrels once in a while.

Alma remembered Henry, her grandpa, called her "babe." She liked the nickname.

Alma loved the enamel tub at her grandmother Lizzie's boarding house. Her grandma said to wash it really good before she took a bath because the boarders used it.

Alma remembered Daphne had $1.00 to spend on each kid for Christmas. She got a xylophone that she didn't like much. She said that Nona was there and wanted Grandma to buy her something too. She didn't have enough money and felt bad that she couldn't.

(Alma wrote) I remember my first job at $1.23 per day working in the hay.

Joe had a pet lamb, and one day while he was at school Cliff cut off its tail. Joe was terribly sad about it. Many years later when Cliff reminded him of the incident, Joe said, "I forgive you Dad." "Do you honey?" Cliff asked back. It's a bittersweet story that

Cliff still had pangs about something that happened so long ago and really wanted to apologize for it.

Lois remembered when Joe's shoes got too small and worn out that her folks threw them in the fire. Joe saw them and was heartbroken, "Oh my little shoes!"

When Lois was young, she fell on the ice and cut her cheek. Cliff lifted her up to show her in the mirror. She thought it looked just like a red willow leaf. Cliff and Daphne held it together with some 1 cent stamps. It healed fine.

One time Joe was bugging big brother George. George had taken all he could, so after warning him, he would throw him in the creek, he did. Joe came up sputtering and swore, "As soon as I get big enough, I'm going to throw you in the creek!"

Henry, Leslie, Alma
Lois, George

Alma remembered the first time she wore pants. Uncle John's sister had a Girl Scout troop that she brought up to the hills. Nona and mom were invited to stay overnight with the group. Mom was in her teens. She borrowed a pair of pants from one of her brothers. They slept in the schoolhouse and hiked up over the hill the next morning.

Les was too young to be included by Henry and George, so he was paired with younger Alma. (Alma wrote) *He even slapped me once when he was fed up with me. This broke my heart. Finally, of course, Mom talked him into apologizing and made everything right again.*

Les would sometimes disappear for some time, like the time our Grandfather Webb visited and Mom took a picture of him with her boys. That is, all except Les.

Les was quite one to experiment with different things. One time he poured some gas on the ground in front of our house and lit a match to it. It made a big fire and had to be fought to keep our house from catching fire.

The Kids Almost Grown

(Alma wrote) *Dad and Uncle John had gone to town one day and came back with everything needed for our baseball team. However, we were a little short on manpower. I dated Stub Quinn who had played shortstop on the Aldridge baseball team. Joe was still too young to play, likewise Bob Dial. Fred Feilding came from the homestead he was proving up on, and he was really good. He had played on a professional team in Utah. He and a few other temporary fellows from the valley helped us out and we played Firth and Goshen and Upper Presto. We had a lot of fun. Bishop Cortez Tenshson showed Russell exactly how to deliver a pitch (with a wind up). Dad and Uncle John, Russ, George, Henry, Les, Fred Fielding, Stub and a Hunter fellow from Firth were the regulars. Stub was short, Fred Fielding was really tall! It was a kind of weird looking bunch. Dad had played baseball on a team from the valley before he was married, and so according to the boys, that was the reason he wanted to play. Anyway, we women had fun going to watch and cheer. Our playing field was on the Johnston Flat. George and Henry played on the Idaho Falls Outlaw team the next year or two before army days.*

Daphne would save up money from the Post Office and they would order lengths of cloth from Montgomery Ward. (Alma wrote) *Being 6 years older, Lois and I were never real chummy. But when we both grew up we made matching clothes for each other.*

(Alma wrote) *It was the fall of 1937 that Les, Nona and I started our junior year at Firth. We walked to school but sometimes got rides. The second year we had two rooms in a house by the canal so it wasn't far. (They had two bedrooms, a kitchenette, with an outhouse). Two lady teachers also roomed there. One was a tall lady who was quite plain, taught geometry and other math subjects and had only 2 or 3 changes of attire. The other was a giddy blonde who taught cooking etc. wore short dresses and a lot of jewelry. I took cooking classes and homemaking from her.*

Henry, George and Russell had a cedar post business for a while. They would cut them, send them down the river, and retrieve them at the Cove. Dad said it didn't work very well, they didn't get all they sent down. During this endeavor, George had an accident and cut a huge gash in his leg. They had to make a hurried trip to the valley.

While Mom, Les and Nona were staying in Firth going to school, Les got blood poisoning. She can't remember a wound, or the symptoms, except for the vein line running up his leg. She was scared and since they were living alone, had to get help from the neighbors, the Lyons. It was a horrible snowy, stormy day and cars couldn't travel. The Lyons hooked up a team and wagon or sled, and Mom rode with Les in the back while the neighbor drove them to Shelley. The doctor sent Les home to stay down and Mom stayed out of school to care for him.

(Alma wrote) *At the time kids starting high school might be "initiated" mostly by sophomores. Several of those characters busted into the rooms where we were staying and they took Les out in the Lavas someplace and left him and fought with Henry. Later that night they brought Les back. Henry had to go to the Dr. and from then on had a bad wrist to deal with while he worked various places for room and board while he finished high school. Les had gone to the Alridge School for 2 extra years while he waited for me and our cousin Nona Dial to finish the 10th grade, so we could all stay together at Firth and finish high school. Mr. Heath was accredited to teach through 10th grade.*

Cliff was bothered by hay fever. The doctor told him it may help if he started smoking. When he caught George smoking, he told him it was a slovenly habit and hoped he was smart enough to end it.

Alma had a pair of riding pants, "jompers." They had the full thigh cut. She loved them. Mom didn't remember what happened to them. Daphne had given them to Helen McBride. Many years later Helen, Bill Webb's daughter, told Mom how much she appreciated them. Helen didn't have much money at the time.

After Mom and Dad died, we found this ledger book kept by Daphne for the year 1943.

Dairy cows	6	Potatoes	20 acres
Yearlings	8	Beans	1 acre
Calves	2	Grazing land	1066 acres
Stock cattle	10	Alfalfa Hay and seed	100 acres
Horses	9	Corn	1 acre
Pigs	100	Peas	½ acre
Sows	11	Orchard	1 ½ acres
Turkeys	30	Dry farm idle	560 acres
Hens	60	Grain	200 acres
Sugar beets	16 acres		

*100 dry farm grain

George on accordion, Les on the fiddle, Henry and Alma on guitar

Clifford and Lois (Alma made her dress)

Mom played in a band with her brothers and cousin, Nona. Henry played the guitar with a harmonica strapped on, Les the fiddle, Nona the accordion and Mom the guitar. They sometimes played with Dale and Zane Mann from Rigby. (Dale later married Deloy Mecham). The Jemmetts played at weddings and dances at Lower Presto, and remembered playing at a dance in Bone all night. Mom can't remember that they had a band name, maybe Cedar Creek or the Jemmett kids. They didn't get paid much. They had dances at the little school house every week for a while, but valley people started coming and kind of ruined it and they quit, but for a while it was fun.

Cliff played the button accordion; Daphne played the accordion and guitar.

Mom would have been valedictorian and Nona the salutatorian if they had taken all their classes at Firth. But since they started as juniors they were excluded from the running.

Mom's best friend in high school was Sylvia Hanson, whom she nicknamed Swamy. She later became Mom's sister-in-law when she married George after their spouses died.

Mom had a job taking care of an invalid woman in Firth for some time after she graduated. She was proud after this woman's son went to the mountains to tell Cliff and Daphne that they really appreciated her work.

When Daphne had a new baby Jean, and Lou died with the appendicitis, she appreciated the nurses so much and wanted Mom to learn nursing. Mom went to interview for training in Idaho Falls. She could tell the women knew she didn't want to be a nurse, and was turned down.

Alma wanted to go to a secretarial school in Salt Lake. She was given a scholarship ($25) when she graduated high school in '39, but she was needed at home and couldn't use it. She finally did go to Henegers, a secretarial school in Salt Lake and enjoyed the training. Alma could write in shorthand for life. She thought having a job working accounts would have been fun.

As people left the area, the school at Cedar Creek was threatened to close. Teacher Clarice Mattson brought her kids to Alridge to keep the school open one year. (Daphne wrote) *They let me teach them the first winter, then the next I stayed with my mother here in the old rock house while Cliff stayed in the hills, caring for the ranch and post office.*

It was about 2 more years before the Post office was disposed of and Clifford also left the Hills. During school season, Daphne stayed with Jean and Bill, but in the summer, they would go to Gibbonsville where Cliff and George were mining. Bill and Jean tried their hands at panning gold. Daphne also did a little fishing for steelhead there.

The Heartbreak of Dry Farming

(Alma wrote) *Dry farming didn't pay very well. I remember the big teams of horses they used. Everything was so hard, pitching hay on a wagon and rolling it off.*

(In a newspaper interview) *Despite their happiness together the years were economically harsh, Cliff said. We had crickets and grasshoppers, hailstorm and drought every year. Everything they could think of they threw at us. We'd never have moved away if we'd had a little cooperation from the weather. I can't understand it" he said. "It's cooperated with them fellers up there every year since."*

The dry farmers gradually began moving away and the Jemmetts started farming their neighbors' land too. When the population dropped so low the school was closed, the Jemmetts left as well.

(*Morning News* interview with Russell) *Russell Jemmett was born and grew up in the little community of Alridge on Cedar Creek, a short distance from the Blackfoot River south of Wolverine on a 4,000-acre dry farm.*

Henry and Clifford bought a header at the Shelley Merc which was pushed by six head of horses. It was easy for that many and they could go all day. They had three horse-drawn header boxes so they kept the header going or tried to. Of course, the grain had to be pitched off the boxes into a stack and then pitched into the thresher. When they got a combine, it was pulled by twelve horses. At one time the Jemmetts had 24 head of horses in harness.

(Russell wrote) *They worked a lot of horses, so had the barn and corrals at Clifford's and big feed mangers. One year they had a real big crop of colts. They were all halter broke and when they were working the mothers they would tie the colts up, what a beautiful sight they were. The next year brain fever hit that part of the country and they lost most all the horses. All that didn't die weren't any good to work or ride. That's what you call hard times and bad luck.*

One year they threshed all the grain from Wolverine to Brush Creek.

(Alma wrote) *Russell went to school through the 6th grade when his parents moved to Shelley during the school year. He remembers the fall that made his dad pull up stakes and move to Mud Lake. Dry farming seemed good then and the big Altman – Taylor tractor had been bought, because the work horses had almost all died from the sleeping sickness. With this giant tractor, a great deal of land had been farmed into wheat, including the Wolverine Bench, the grain was looking great, was 'in the boot' when an early frost hit, the grain was killed, only dry stalks which soon blew away so the ground looked like it had never been planted. Such was the farmer's life.*

When Henry left, Alma said that from then on, Clifford and John Dial were partners and always good friends, both cheerful optimistic fellows.

(Russell wrote) *Uncle Scaley and Aunt Em had moved to Shelley a number of years before Mother and Dad. After Mother and Dad left the Cove, it seemed like it just started to wither up and die and when Dad left the last time, it seemed to finish it off, it never was the same again.*

Henry and Lois lived in the Cove house before she died. When George returned from war, he, Millie and baby Tony lived in the Cove house. Henry and Ruby, Josie and Ed (Butch) lived with them. Edward still remembers living there. He said baby Wayne was born while they lived there too. The other kids were born after they moved to Wapello. Mom said various family members lived in the Cove for a while and can't remember when it was abandoned for good. Henry made a wooden replica of the cove house.

We're not sure now what happened to the partnership between Cliff and John Dial. Not long after Cliff and Daphne moved to Blackfoot, John sold the Cove place and caused hard feelings with the Jemmett family as several members would have loved a chance at it. We do know that Elsie and John Dial continued to be very good friends with Cliff and Daphne throughout their lives.

The new owner blasted the rocks through the canyon to make the road down Cedar Creek wide enough for a combine. Cliff said, "Well, with all those rocks pushed over, when the spring flood came down it didn't have no place to go so it washed out the whole road."

The road was never rebuilt. The cabin can only be reached now on foot, down a mile of narrow trail that hugs the cliff in places, and winds along and sometimes through Cedar Creek.

The Cove was and still is a cherished piece of history that was lost to the family. The house, at the bottom of the bluff and out of reach of vandals, still stands, but curious cattle walk in and out now, and the river is washing nearer and nearer to the building.

After the Move to Blackfoot

In Blackfoot, Cliff and Daphne, their hair now silvered by age, look dreamily down 71 years of married life to the little cabin on The Cove and their house in Lonesome Hollow. "We were the happiest there," Daphne said. "I wish we'd never had to leave."

The rock house in Blackfoot where they lived for the rest of their lives was a wonderful place. It hid in an alcove, away from traffic and neighbors and hidden by trees. It had a huge garden where Cliff could raise berries, and a cool cellar for Daphne to work her clay. Even the train running close by was magical to us, growing up away from big town life.

There were many comforts, like flushing toilets, electricity and water from a tap in Blackfoot. Someone asked Daphne if she missed living in those beautiful hills and she answered, "Not a bit!"

Cliff and Daphne and John and Elsie Dial spent happy days on the river or the Blackfoot reservoir fishing. Daphne would come home with a fresh batch of cold sores, but believed it was worth it for she loved the Hills.

After this time with most of her children grown, she had time for her love of writing poems and short stories, many of which were published. She published a volume of poetry and songs, *Sunshine and Shadows.* My mother Alma published *The Silent One*, a historical romance written by Daphne and based on a true story of someone she knew about that was gored in the throat by his oxen and lived with a serious disability.

Daphne had a job with the newspaper writing about people and events illustrating them with photos she took. While contributing to all the area newspapers, Blackfoot, Shelley, Idaho Falls, Pocatello, Boise and Salt Lake City, she spent many hours researching and writing about Bingham County's colorful beginnings. Her weekly columns "Over the Back Fence" in the *Blackfoot Bulletin* and "The Blackfoot Scene" in the Pocatello *Journal* ran for several years.

(Granddaughter Lorna wrote) *They (her columns) had bits of poetry, literature, scripture, history, some politics, some people watching and lots of good old fashioned common sense. She had a weekly radio show on KBLI for a while talking about current events and the history of the area. Her finger was on the pulse of Bingham County and she shared it with her readers and listeners. She named names. And by that I mean she recognized the ordinary people that she met and visited with. Their actions may not have been earth shaking, but they were important, and Daphne gave them their moment to shine.*

As Daphne got older and her health failed, she gave up the newspaper job. Her chief pleasure then was working with native clay making beautiful pottery and character figurines.

I got a little, (about 3 inch) clay papoose for a birthday present. She rolled a ball for the head, painted a face on it, and wrapped a small piece of flannel for the body all fashioned on a clay papoose board. It survived our house fire and has been glued. But I treasure it. Another family favorite are the pencil holders. She would put long john fabric in a container and push the clay into it. After it dried, it would have the knubby pattern of the underwear fabric and wrinkles making a unique and artistic jar. We all have one of these pencil holders. She had a potter's wheel and kiln but most of her work was done with her hands.

Alma, George and Henry developed an Alridge memorial and small park near the first school and on the site of the Alridge Post Office and home kept by Daphne and Clifford Jemmett. They got a huge rock which Henry inscribed and had a nice iron fence built around it anchored in cement to keep the cattle out. They made a fire pit and installed a nice picnic table in hopes people would stop and sit. One day my sister and her husband were driving by to reach their cattle in the mountains, when they came upon a wedding ceremony being conducted under the elm in the park – complete with an audience seated around the couple!

Alma and her brothers were also instrumental in getting the Alridge school restored and moved to the Shelley Park. It is a wonderful place with other buildings moved from their locations too. People can picnic and enjoy buildings from another era.

Through Daphne's working years and Cliff's berry business, they saved enough money to give each of their kids $3, 865 when they died.

They died in 1987, Daphne first in April, Cliff following in September.

Cliff and Daphne have been featured in several newspaper articles describing their lives and their long, loving marriage over the years, anniversaries of 60 years, 64, 68, 70 and 74. Mom had saved these.

Inside the interviews are clues to their relationship. "Anyone could stay married to someone as wonderful as my husband." Daphne said with a shy smile.

"Clifford has always been so agreeable; he always said 'Anything you want is fine with me.'"

Cliff said many times when he talked of his descendants, "Not a bad one in the bunch!"

In a letter to a grandchild, Daphne wrote, "Honey, I can't think of a better wish for you than that you find a mate as fine as your grandfather, or your own father, and children as good and fine as ours." She went on to tell about when one of her boys was about to leave for military service and asked her, "Mother, what do you expect of us boys? What do you want us to do?" She told him that it didn't matter a great deal... as long as he did his best in whatever he was doing... as long as it was decent.

(Alma wrote) *Daphne was so very proud of her children and grandchildren and always let them know it. Until the last few years when her mind became so befuddled, there was never a more kind and caring person. Her life's philosophy was "Just be decent." She thought that said it all and I think so too. She has been an inspiration.*

Bill, Les, Alma, Jean, Joe, Daphne, George, Cliff, Lois, Henry

Five Simple Rules on How to be Happy, though Married

By Daphne Jemmett

Dear Grandchild and new Spouse,

My husband and I have been married for a long, long time. Our Golden wedding has come and the years have piled up since that time. However, we are still on speaking terms. We can laugh together and enjoy each other's company. While we can't claim that it has been easy, it has been richly rewarding. I think one can honestly call it a good, lasting marriage.

During the years together we acquired a fine lot of grandchildren and right here I might add that we are proud of every one of them. Some are married with growing families of their own. Others have recently married, while still others have indicated that they will embark on the sea of matrimony in the near future. It isn't only the bride and groom to whom I want to point out these signposts to a long and contented married life, but to all the grandchildren who have already married and to those who will do so in the future, that I am speaking wherever they are, or whatever they are doing...and I hope some of them are listening

Knowing how easy it is to lose the way to a happy ending, we have compiled five easy rules on how to be happy – though married. They are:

1- Don't yell at each other.
2- Don't blow your top.
3- Do talk seriously together.
4- Do learn to listen.
5- Don't forget to remember.

Let's take the first one - Don't yell at each other. That is not in anger or complaint. We've seen so much happiness frightened away by loud complaining voices. Oh, it's fine to goof around and make a lot of noise in fun. It brightens the days when things get dismal. But don't raise your voice in anger. It's so useless and it never settles or solves anything.

Number two - Don't blow your top. We all know that the broad field of everyday living is dedicated to a great extent by necessity. There is so much to do and little annoyances crop up constantly. You can't avoid them; they come built in like the weather. It is so easy to blame someone else when things go wrong, and even easier to become angry when you feel you're being blamed for something that may or may not have been you fault. That's when little annoyances have a way of flaring up into big trouble, and when, if you can't manage to cool it, you may be in trouble, maybe big trouble. For big annoyances often mushroom into great clouds of resentment that might go BOOM like an atomic bomb. And maybe take your promising marriage with it. And if *the marriage did manage to survive it wouldn't be as good a marriage as before. Oh it might drag along for years, but the nice feel of togetherness, the good will and affection would eventually dry up and disappear. So, when you feel like blowing your top, DON"T! Think awhile. Think quite awhile. You know it might be that you were partly to blame in the first place.*

Rule number three – Do talk seriously together. This rule is especially applicable when making any decision that concerns you both. When you have a problem (And who doesn't occasionally) try and find a neutral spot in your thinking and bring it out in the open and look at it from all angles and discuss it together, applying rule number four.

Rule number four – Do learn to listen. Now it is very important to keep your listening ears wide open. And it does little good if any, for one to do all the talking and the other to merely listen. It must be a joint affair, with each stating their views and also doing their share of listening. Then when you have discussed the problem over calmly, resolve the decision together. This advice to talk things over, is to our minds Important enough that it should be incorporated into each marriage ceremony. It is the real give and take of a marriage. It isn't enough to be able to give, or give in willingly, one must also be able to accept graciously and with appreciation.

Rule number five is probably the most important one of all - Don't forget to remember. Don't forget to remember what? Don't forget that each of you is an individual in your own right. You are married now. You are a family. You belong together. But you don't own each other! We think this is important enough to repeat. You belong together, but you don't own each other!

My husband tells me that I could have said all this in a lot fewer words, probably he is right; but at any rate.

From both of us: Today you are starting down what we hope will be a long and happy life together. Children, love each other, be kind to each other. Work together, play together, be happy. And may the good Lord bless you both.

Trapping and Hunting Stories

Cliff and Lois with some of his furs

(Henry Jemmett wrote about trapping for the Bingham County History book) *My father (Cliff) has told me that as a boy riding through the mountains with his father (Henry) he saw many large beaver dams that had been worked and lived in for centuries. As the dam filled with silt it would be built higher and higher. Some of them covered many acres. As a caretaker it was Henry's job to control the population of beavers. In the season of 1955 and 1956, he worked with his dad Cliff. They started in early Oct 1955, and ended the middle of November 1956, with a take of 250 beaver pelts. They also trapped several mink, around 50 muskrats and two bobcats.*

(Russell wrote) *Me and my nephew George headed for the hills trapping. We had more fun than a nose bleed. I've had more fun and enjoyment all by myself on top of those mountains than any place I've ever been. My brother Clifford had the post office at Alridge and somehow I got the job packing the mail to Firth and back twice a week. It worked in well with my trapping. I worked at that for several years. We had a lot of good trapping in the fall and spring, there were beaver dams on Brush Creek and Rawlins Creek, you could have used a boat. There was always a lot of rats and mink to work on, and there wasn't all the people to contend with now. There are more people in the winter due to the snow machines. It was a snowshoe show then and that really weeds the men from the boys. We had our ups and downs but we always had some fur to sell. We sure never got rich but we always had a barrel of fun.*

The boys trapped muskrat, but later beaver and coyote, sometimes they happened to get a mink, which was cause for celebration.

(Alma wrote) *One day George, Henry and Russell tracked a wolf all day and evening and didn't ever catch up to him. (this was the only one they ever saw) Daphne was worried when they didn't show up for lunch and then dinner.*

(Alma wrote) *I remember my dad and the boys skinning their game and stretching the hides on frames. George, Henry and Russell would take off on skis and be gone all day checking or putting out trap lines.*

(Russell wrote) *Clifford had a dog he called Ring. He was a good trap line dog, if a coyote would get away with a trap, Ring would soon round him up. The sheep men and government trappers were scattering poison all over the hills. Ring got in the bait and died. Clifford always hated poison.*

(Russell wrote) *Cliff was trapping gophers around the garden. He caught a weasel, as he trapped them in the winter, he decided to turn it loose. He stepped on the spring of the trap to release him, but the old weasel was kind of mad having been treated that way and all. He ran up his leg and bit him on the finger. Once they bite, they really hang on and he had a hell of a time to get loose from it. He had a sore finger for quite a while and every one he caught after that he hoped was the one that bit him.*

(Russell wrote) *Clifford had his own Fourth of July and it wasn't anywhere close to the fourth. He did quite a lot of hunting along with his trapping and would load his own shells. One night he had loaded quite a while and decided to call it a day. He said he had the prettiest bunch of cats and his old dog lying around him; the cats a purring and old dog snoring. He had spilled a few grains of powder and when he was cleaning up he touched a match to it. He saw a little red speck go up in the air and was headed right for his powder sack, he fell over backwards in a big old wood box. About that time all hell broke loose. The dog was barking, the cats were a squalling and running up and down the walls, some of the shells he had loaded exploded. He said he thought the world had come to an end.*

All his beautiful cats took to the hills; only one of them ever showed up again and that was the next spring. One day Cliff came in and saw the old cat looking around the corner of the cabin just like he didn't know if it was safe or what to expect. (Earlier this cat lost a leg in a trap, but lived a long time afterwards, he was named appropriately Crip.)

(Russell wrote) *George and I left Miner Creek one morning about day light and when the sun started to come up, we found we had left our sunglasses back at the cabin. By the time we got back we were almost snow blind. We washed our eyes out with salt water the rest of the day and we were ready to try it again come morning.*

(Interview with Russell) He slept under the stars when the weather was good but when a storm would make getting back to their headquarters a risk, they headed for one of the line camp cabins that were sprinkled throughout the hills. "They weren't much" he said "Sometimes you could sit and watch the snow drifting across the floor". If they happened to have a little food on them, they had supper. If not, they slept hungry. "I guess it was cold, but it didn't seem cold. It was a good life." Russell said with a sigh as he looked at photos of his beaver, fox, coyote, mink and muskrat and other pelts. "I trapped about anything that had fur." he said "I made more money trapping than (anything else) I ever did in my life."

(Russell wrote) George and I used to travel on skis a lot of the time. He was better on them than I was, so he would break trail over the rough spots. One day, we came out of High Basin and if you worked it right you could ride right down to the cabin door. It had been a while since we had been over it and the wind had been blowing and it had iced over in a few spots. George went first and he waved when he hit the bottom. Well, being as I had to get all the speed I could to coast over the next rise, I turned them loose. Lord have Mercy, I was just about ready to break the sound barrier when I hit the first ice; I know I was a good fifty feet off the ground. Well, I made that one and had just got things about under control when I hit the next one. Well, George said I made three complete somersaults in the air before I came down. I found I didn't have any broken bones and rode down to the cabin door. I had my snow shoes in the cabin so I got the axe and took the skies to the chopping block and cooked super with them. That was the last time I was ever on a pair of skis.

Henry trapped the country in the hills for many years. One year he trapped a cougar in his bobcat trap. The 135 lb. male cougar had dragged the trap about 100 yards from where the trap was set close to where Cedar Creek empties into the Blackfoot River. Henry had never trapped or even seen a cougar there before. He was so excited he stopped at the *Blackfoot News*. Daphne was disappointed he didn't go to her house so she could have scooped the story. This same trip they also caught 3 bobcats. That winter they trapped 36 bobcats.

(Russell wrote) One spring I started for Rawlins Creek for the spring break up to do some rat trapping. I took a short cut and came out right above the cabin. We had a lot of snow that winter and it had drifted to the point where there was a big hang over. I went down the ridge till I thought I could make it. Well, the snow started to slide and it had drifted right over a quaky patch. I had quite a pack with my grub and traps and when I got stopped my snow shoes were hung in a quaky tree and I was head down in one hell of a fix. The more I tried, the more straight up and down I was, with my snow shoes tied on solid. I finally got out of my pack sack and got loose from the quaky tree. For a time, I was starting to feel like a trapped coyote.

John Dial, Russell, Cliff, George

(Russell wrote) *I was headed for Miner Creek one morning checking a few traps on the way. The wind was a blowing and it was snowing, regular damn blizzard. I looked over the bluff along the river and there stood a beautiful coyote, it was a good big twenty-dollar bill so I shot it. It looked like it was done for so I worked my way down over the rocks and was almost to it when it started to crawl in the rocks. I got there just in time to grab him by the tail. He was one mad coyote. I couldn't get him out of the rocks. I had some extra pack laces so I tied him up by the tail. I thought he would be dead when I came by the next day, when I got there the next day, he was still alive and madder than before. But I was prepared, I got him out and it was one more pelt to add to the collection.*

(Russell wrote) *We had a trapping cabin on Miner Creek. One morning I stirred up a batch of hot cakes. I had some honey in a fruit jar and that was what I had to have on them cakes. I went to take the lid off and the jar broke and it cut my hand and wrist pretty bad. It cut an artery in my wrist so I put a tourniquet on my arm and twisted it up tight and headed for the ranch to get it sewed up. I had about 10 miles to go and those snow shoes got heavy before I got there. My brother Clifford took me to town. I didn't get there until late in the afternoon. It took quite a few stitches to stop the bleeding. But it sure put a stop to having honey in a fruit jar.*

(Alma wrote) *Dad and Uncle John were hunting up the old Lockyear Hollow. The younger guys had crawled over the fence and walked up further to hunt. This was after Dad and Mom had moved to the valley. At the end of the hollow, top of the hill, Dad saw 2 big buck deer and shot them both. They went back to get something to haul them in from Uncle John's. The young guys had got a doe and a fawn. Dad was pleased to remember about it and how good he did.*

One time Henry was bow hunting and sitting very still. He was in camouflage and on a narrow trail. An elk came up behind and almost stepped on him. George had a similar experience. He was watching out across the valley and an elk came slowly in back of him and sniffed his shoulder.

(Russell wrote about his dog) *We had been through hell and high water together. I thought he would take up with my brother when I left for the army but he wouldn't have anything to do with anyone. Clifford said he would just lay and look down the road waiting for me to come home. I guess he just roamed the hills looking for me, got in poison bait and died. What a tear jerker that was. I know he will be waiting in the sweet bye and bye. A year or so later I got up one morning and there was a big Airedale dog lying on my floor. It was late in the fall and the sheep and cattle were coming out of the hills and I thought someone had lost him, but I never could find anyone he belonged to. He turned out to be a great trap line dog. He could stand flat footed and whip a coyote and you couldn't catch him in a trap. I had him two or three years and I woke up one morning and he was gone like he came in the night. I never saw hide or hair of him again.*

Cliff and Russell

(Russell wrote about his brother Cliff) *He has passed on now but he was very special to me. In all the years, I never saw him mad, the Lord knows he had enough to make him mad at times. I have tried to copy my life the way he lived his. He loved wildlife and became a very good trapper and as I grew up, I remember the beautiful furs he had. I guess that's the reason I live for every fur season to roll around for I get so much enjoyment out of the trap line. I have almost starved to death doing it, but I always had a million dollars' worth of fun.*

The War Years

Fred, Alma, unknown, Ruby, Henry, Millie with Jean, George

Daphne's very earliest reporting was a little carbon copied weekly newspaper written during the World War II years, "*The Alridge Chronicle.*" It was single spaced, both sides, and typed with a carbon to save time. It furnished news to and about the local boys in the service. She sent them to her own three sons, Les, George, and Joe, brother-in-law Russell, and son-in-law Fred Reid. There were lots of men, neighbors, friends and more distant relatives in the area so everyone was kept abreast of one another. Cliff didn't like FDR because all his boys served in the war.

This is a photo of one page of The Chronicle. I have retyped the issue for easier reading on the following pages. The letter "C" was bent on her manual typewriter.

Vol. I   **THE ALRIDGE CHRONICLE**   April 13, 1945

Owned and Edited by Clifford Jemmett
Associate Editor, Daphne Jemmett
Reporters, Nona Dial and Betty Polson
'Lo Folks

Just to make sure that we don't forget it again, here is the prayer sent to us to send to you, by our old friend and neighbor, Pearl Brown.**********??????????Where the dickens IS IT? I guess this is an April Fool on us--we can't find the copy--so here we AREN'T again.

Well, anyway, we DO have some news.

Bob has been home on leave for almost a week. He came up from Pocatello where he had picked up Thelma, Bud, and the three boys, and here he came and surprised the folks, who'd not expected him for another week at least. BOY, was it ever good to see him, and HAS he got a cute gal—he's had her up; here in Alridge a whole lot this week, and we are all very glad to get acquainted with her.

A couple of hours ago, they came to the office of the Chronicle to bid us goodby. It will seem doubly lonesome now.

Seaman Bob goes back to San Diego to get in some more training. Good luck, Bob.

Also we heard from S/Sgt. Leslie T. Jemmett who seems to be back in France at the minute, and you can never tell from one minute to the next where that lad will be. He relieves our mind quite a bit--it seems as if the building in the picture (see our Mar. II issue) is NOT a barracks but only a temporary work shop they made out of a German trailer. It's surely nice to know that Tarz is all O.K. Somehow we'd worried quite a lot about him.

And as Leslie is back in France, Russell is on to Germany. It doesn't seem as if the two of them will ever get together. Russ says that he is having as much fun as if he had his right mind, and for us not to worry and that he thinks it won't be long before he is home again. We just knew that when both Les and Russ were on the job over there that we'd get results---some sort of results, anyway.

Sg. George seemed just a little depressed in his last letter. It's my opinion that where he is would depress anyone. Won't it be swell, folks, when this is over and ALL of our boys are back.

We sent for that information, son, but told them to send it direct to you, as we thought you would get it sooner that way. Perhaps you have it already. George is interested in Alaska, folks, I guess that a little cold and snow would seem good down there in the tropics.

Pvt. Joe Paul is out on Biviouc, so news form is sorta' scant. However, we are hoping to see him on furlough soon.

We are sure that Pvt. Larry Polson will be pleased to see friend Wifie when she arrives at Camp Wolters. Betty insists that she IS going as soon as possible.

Reed Baird and Forrest Hunter of Firth were both on Iwo Jima, and we think they both got through it O.K. Also one of Ez Johnson's sons was there, too, on a ship. Reed got to talk to him, but we aren't sure which one of Ex's sailer sons it was.

It was with mixed emotions that the citizens of Alridge heard of the death of the commander-in-chief of the Army and Navy. We all wish all the success in the world to attend the efforts of President Truman. Long may he live, well may he prosper, and we hope to heck he does as well by the people of the U.S. One Nation, one people, with liberty & justice for all.

Not to change the subject, but our editor is very busy just now, making a fruit cupboard for the cellar, here at the post office. More power to him, and we hope he doesn't hit a finger or a thumb.

We were all set to go and see if the Reids were still ticking, but received a letter from Mrs. Fred, so we didn't have to.

The senior Reids went on a trip awhile back with the Henry Williams of Firth. They were to visit in Portland, Oregon at the home of Mr. Reid's brother, Don, and then proceed to Wash. To visit relative there, however, Mr. Reid's health made it advisable to cancel the Wash. Visit. They are staying on in Portland, where Bob is trying one more cure for asthma.

The Senior Play was presented last Wed. at the Firth High School. Doug had a leading part, and we'll bet a cookie that it was well worth seeing.

The Reids have a pressure water system installed now---a dandy, too.

Did you all know that Firth has a newspaper? Well, she sho' has. It was started sometime along about Christmas, and from that time to this it has been improving itself until we are afraid it will even exceed the Chronicle in appeal, if it doesn't watch out. Its official name is "The Firth Record" and Dad went in and subscribed for it all by himself. We have just received one copy so far, but we enjoyed it very much. The rumor has it that the Lion's Club put in a subscription for the service men in the vicinity, so you may have received copies yourselves. If you don't get it, just say so and we will see to it that you do. By the way, the Editor of the Record is old BOOZIE'S nephew. He's been all over "these parts".

The younger Engstrums have moved back to Alridge for the summer. They are both looking hale and hearty. It looks like life in the big wicked city agrees with them.

Thelma and the three boys are here at the Ranch, have been ever since they brought Bob home last Sat. Thelma came up and brought us news of the President's death--we'd been house cleaning and had missed it entirely.

The little boys surely do enjoy it here at Grandpa's. Dennis saw a "Hen" laying some goose eggs--"GREAT BIG ONES, GRANDMA", grandma wondered if he wasn't meaning the hen she has setting one goose eggs.

Dennis and Delon are almost of a size, Lonnie a little the tallest and Dennis broad enough to make up for it, while Larry, now just 8 months old is as cute as a bug's ear. You hardly ever see three such cute little dickenses all together. I'll bet Bud and Sammy are proud of them.

Lois writes from Wash. That the house Chet is making is getting to look like a home. Also she says that Mrs. Brown seems to be getting a lot better, and that Mr. Brown says that all of the credit for it belongs to Maurene.

Henry and Ruby and the children are all settled at the Cove, and Henry is trapping beaver under a state permit. GOODNESS, but he has a few big ones. They look like the great grandaddys of all beavers.

The spring house cleaning is on in full blast in Alridge, both on Cedar Creek and the Blackfoot River. The women folks are taking advantage of the bad weather to get it done before the men start the spring plowing and planting. By the way, there's the last year's crop of alfalfa to thresh, too. It has been almost dry enough several times, and then comes ANOTHER STORM.

The Buffalo Skull that has grazed the rock garden at the P.O. for so many years has finally fallen apart—oh, well, what did we want with a Buffalo Skull, anyway?

Things are beginning to show a little green, but they do so grudgingly, as if spring wasn't certain of its welcome. Well, as long as all our April showers are snow storms, what can she (it) expect anyway.

So Long, Everybody. We'll be with you again next week.
THE STAY-AT-HOMERS

Love Daphne

World War II Veterans

George Jemmett

(Russell wrote) *We were in the hills when the Japs bombed Pearl Harbor so we didn't know anything about it for a few days. George went out to the ranch and was going to be back in a day or two. He didn't show up so I went out hunting him, thinking he might have got in trouble. Hell, he had joined the army and was ready to settle a score or two with the Japs.*

He was on the California coast for about a year and a half with Millie before he shipped out. (Interview with George for the Blackfoot News) *George put his prowess earned as a pitcher on the family team to use on the Army's baseball team and met one of the United State's greatest ball players of all time- Joe DiMaggio.*

The Army sent their celebrity team to play us. He said "He hit a home run off me but I still got to say that I struck out Joe DiMaggio."

His pitching arm stood George in good stead another time, a time that was a matter of life and death.

"The Japanese were attacking us and they sent me and another guy to a little knoll in front of our front line with a couple of boxes of hand grenades. Our job was to keep the Japanese from getting to the high ground."

As his helper handed him grenades, standing beside a concrete pillar George pulled the pins and lobbed them with deadly accuracy at the charging enemy soldiers.

He threw until the cases were empty and the concrete pillar was reduced to rebar by gunfire, but the Americans held their ground.

George says he learned to pray on the island of Okinawa, when his company of 140 men was reduced to 7 by the horrific battles they engaged in

On Okinawa my comrades were being taken daily; sometimes many of them at a time.

"My best friend came to me and said he'd been hit in the back by shrapnel. I walked him to the aid station and left him. When I came back to see how he was, he was dead."

They had talked of Alaska and mining gold after the war, George said with teary eyes. "We had it all figured out. I could see where he was hit and I didn't really think there was anything that bad wrong with him, but they couldn't fix it.

He was wounded twice himself - stabbed in the thigh by a bayonet-wielding enemy soldier, and shot in the right hand. Both wounds healed without benefit of hospitalizations, his only treatment daily dressings by medics. There was no hospitals to go to", he said simply.

Wherever he was, pencil and notebook were never far from his hand, and he expressed his thoughts in poetry, whether about the horror and waste of war, or longing for home and family.

He later published a couple of books of poetry.

George had enough points for discharge before the war ended and was headed home aboard a troop ship with two purple hearts and a bronze star when he heard the Japanese had surrendered.

He was discharged at Ft. Lewis, Wash., and caught a bus home, but finding he had a night's layover in Boise, struck out hitchhiking. "Right outside of town a couple from Pocatello picked me up. They took me right to my wife's parents house there.

(Daphne wrote) George saw the worst of the WWII action; he served in islands around Japan in the army.

He served about 4 1/2 years without coming home. He saw some terrible fighting and had the closest calls. He had a saber sword he retrieved from a Japanese solider that had committed Harri karri (suicide).

George came upon a 12 x 12 shack in a banana field. The telephone was ringing inside. George went in, picked up the receiver and listened as Japanese talked back and forth. He said "Hello, how are you?" They quit talking. In this shack there was a hide of a snake that went across three walls, it had to be 20 feet long.

One time George found a Japanese soldier sleeping so he captured him. An American soldier came up and shot him point blank killing him. He was jumping around excited shouting "I killed me a Jap!" George yelled at him "I should kill you! He was surrendering!"

Tony was born while George was abroad. Millie named him Tony, George didn't like the name, he knew too many Tonys in the army.

George wrote of many close calls when he knew someone was looking after him. Several times he was prompted to move from where he was sleeping or eating and shortly thereafter a bomb would hit the place he had just left. He woke in the night in a foxhole to someone calling his name. He heard a grenade drop in the fox hole but he couldn't find it to throw it out. His buddy's lost his leg in the blast and took the brunt of the force, but George didn't get hurt. Another time four of his friends were going somewhere and he had the feeling he shouldn't join them. One stepped on a land mine and all were killed.

(Daphne wrote) *Our son George has received the Purple Heart for being wounded in action. It was during an engagement in the battle of Leyte and we are glad to think that it is all ok again now. He is the first of the Alridge soldiers to be given the Purple Heart and we sincerely hope he will be the last.*

(Daphne wrote) *We've got so much good news that we just simply don't know where to start. To begin with we have a letter from Sgt. George Jemmett saying that he is on alert to be sent back to being a Mr. instead of a Sgt. And not to send any more mail until we have another address.*

(Daphne wrote) *Two brothers, George and Les, sons of Clifford Jemmett, of our fair city, arrived home within a day of each other from theaters of War across the globe. Just between you, I and the gate post folks, George looks like a million dollars to us, even if he is kind of thin. Boy, are we glad to have him here. He and Millie are busy fixing up the big room at the Cove.*

When George came home it was hard for all of them to adjust. He didn't want to talk about his experiences for a long time.

Russell Jemmett

To tell the story of Russell's army experience, I have blended excerpts from his own words, "The Life and Travels of the Kid Trapper," and an interview he did with *The Blackfoot News.* Note that the following switches from first person to third person to delineate the two sources.

When Russell Jemmett went off to war in 1942, years of roaming the Blackfoot River Mountains in search of fun and fortune had prepared him well for the physical rigors he would endure. As a young man he earned his living punching cows in the summer and trapping in the winter. He was also used to dining on the simplest of fare. He attributes his surviving the war to the rough and spartan life he led as a youth and pared his 6-foot frame down to rawhide toughness. "We were used to hardship. I think that was one of the reasons I made it back home – all those hard knocks I got up in the hills."

But even the tough life he led growing up couldn't prepare him for a forced march across Germany on one meal a day of bread and cheese while suffering shrapnel wounds to his face. He survived the grueling tour although he dropped 76 pounds and it was 35 years before the Army admitted he had been a prisoner of war.

After Pearl Harbor, I worked and trapped a couple more years before Uncle Sam drafted me. I was sworn into the army at Fort Douglas, Utah, Nov 11, 1943 and they shipped me to Camp Shelby Mississippi.

When we left Fort Douglas, it was ten below and six inches of snow. At Camp Shelby, the grass was green and I froze to death the rest of the winter. In my way of thinking Mississippi is the land that God forgot, there is everything there to make life miserable for a human being. We took our basic training there.

Then they shipped us to leg horn Italy.

(Russell wrote) *The Colosseum was a marvel to the boy from Idaho.* "I read about it in school, but never dreamed I would see it", Jemmett said. "It was an engineering marvel. How they even got the stones up there was a question, let alone how they kept them from falling down. It was worth the war to me just to see it."

There were two kinds of shovel heads to dig foxholes. George and Russell said it didn't take long to dig a hole when you were scared for your life.

I was in E company light machine guns and sixty mortars and we thought we were ready for anything they could dish out. The training we had at Rome really paid off when we hit the Siegfried line, it didn't slow us down. We took a lot of prisoners. They seemed to be glad to get out of it. We were trenching as fast as we could go and not meeting any resistance. It was getting close to Christmas and they were telling us what a wonderful Christmas dinner we were going to have. The German army had a surprise for *us in what they called the Battle of the Bulge. We got in part of it. We lost our Christmas dinner. All we had was K rations which were real welcome.*

Everything was going really well until we hit the Neckar River. There was a little town on the other side of the river. They sent a patrol into the town and they said it was all clear. They let us cross, then they threw everything they had at us, even the kitchen sink. I never saw so many black helmets. I don't know where they all came from but they were there and they kicked the living hell out of us.

With most of their company wiped out, Jemmett, two other men and their sergeant took refuge in an empty factory building, but shelling by the Germans brought it down around their ears. "When the top started to cave in, the sergeant said we had to get out of there. he jumped out and they nearly cut him in half with their machine guns."

Russell felt a blow on the head and suddenly found he couldn't see at all. Believing he was blind he groped his way through darkness and down some stairs behind his two buddies. At the back of the building, they found a cement door that opened to the outside.

"I opened the door and could see light. I was never so happy about anything in my life" he said. He also felt wetness and pain and found his lack of vision was explained. His eyes were filled with blood from wounds in his forehead. "My eyebrows were all shot to hell" he said.

Prisoners

They were lying behind the building watching enemy soldiers dig trenches along the river when Jemmett got an uneasy feeling. He looked over his shoulder and saw 15 to 20 soldiers looking down their rifle barrels at him. "They were just young kids," Jemmett said. "The rifles were pretty near as tall as they were. They were nervous and shaking so badly I was afraid they might shoot us by accident. They kept saying 'All is kaput, all is kaput.'"

(Daphne wrote) Luckily Russ has (only) a small shrapnel scar on his upper lip and had a bullet take a piece out of both trousers legs as it passed between them, burning his flesh as it went. The three from Russ's outfit were taken prisoner by S.S. Troops and were marched back into an area where there were trenches already dug. They were lined up while the S.S. held a confab and Russ says that they had just about decided that they were to be shot right there when the soldiers motioned them on.

The youthful soldiers apparently didn't know what to do with their prisoners. A boy medic cleaned his wounds and instead of taking them to a POW camp their captors simply herded them along in the path of the retreating German army until the war ended. "They picked up other POWs as we went," Jemmett said. "Men that was working on farms, and there was about two hundred of us in the end. We walked clear across Germany to the foot of the Alps in Austria."

As far as I know there were only three of us left out of our company, and we were prisoners. That's when we started walking, seeing the country on foot. My buddy's feet were in really bad shape as we were marching, he would say. "I've got to fallout" and I would cuss hell out of him. When he got mad, he would keep going. I had some extra socks and so did he and whenever we would stop, we would wash his feet and change (socks). His feet were just like five pounds of hamburger, but we finally got them healed up.

They had a big kettle on wheels and that's what they cooked in. One day they had a quarter of horse meat. They got some cabbage and a few potatoes from the old farmer whose barn they had us penned up in. I tell you that was one swell meal. We were always able to find some potatoes in the barns where we stopped. My buddy said, "if I ever get home, I will never sit down to a meal unless I have a side dish of raw potatoes."

They lacked proper clothing and bedding and their lives were made more miserable on that long and painful march by infestations of body lice in their hair and clothing. "They'd stick in our shirts like foxtail in a threshing machine," Jemmett noted. "We picked them off each other, even found lots of uses for them." One was using the lice to determine who would get the occasional cigarette butt they found on the ground. "We'd sit around a table or something and put the cootie in the middle. Whoever it ran to was the winner," he recalled with a grin.

Every morning, they lined us up six deep and gave the lead guy a loaf of black bread and quarter pound circle of cheese that he divided among us. The meager bit of nourishment had to last until the next day, Jemmett said, and the starving men scrounged what they could from the countryside as they marched. Sugar beets and potatoes eaten raw helped sustain them.

We were going through a town we were looking for cigarette butts, shooting sniper as we called it. It's really something how far you can spot one and sometimes you were lucky and no one would spot it before you got there.

A white-haired woman who stood on the street in Munich was passing out pieces of freshly baked bread to the prisoners as they passed. "She had a basket of bread and was cutting off slices and handing them out," Jemmett said. "It was all gone by the time I got there but it stuck in my mind her doing that."

The trek was like a nightmare. One day they marched over forty miles carrying double packs and when one of them gave out the others carried them too.

Their last stop as prisoners was in an empty building, Jemmett said. They were bedded down for the night and the Germans were walking guard around the building when they went to sleep. When they awakened the next morning, their captors had disappeared. The stronger of the men went in search of food and the rest sat against the side of the building in the sunshine to await their fate. It turned out to be the most beautiful day of their lives. They heard a tank approaching and waited with racing hearts. To their immense relief the 3rd Armored Division came rolling around the bend in the road, and they learned the war was over.

"They didn't have any real food, but the driver threw us a carton of cigarettes and some K ration," Jemmett said. The driver also gave them two or three cases of champagne and some coffee. The men who had left to forage returned with some eggs and they celebrated their freedom by washing down the eggs with champagne and coffee, something they hadn't seen in months. We were there for a few days. But we were on full rations once again.

Russell was a prisoner of war for three months from April 6, 1945 to August 9, 1945. They started with the 3 of them, and kept adding more prisoners from the fields where they had been working, until they numbered around 170. They marched constantly and almost reached the border into Austria. Russell was in the war for three years. He weighed 211 when he left and 135 when he was freed.

Russell said it was hard to be a soldier because you were expected to do everything you've been taught your whole life was wrong.

Finally, they loaded us on an old beat-up transport like a bunch of sheep. Some of the boys were sick at their stomach and some had dysentery bad. I know they must have junked that plane when they unloaded us, for I know they could never get it cleaned up. They flew us into Camp Lucky Strike France. We were (in flight) three hours and forty-five minutes and that was the longest three hours I ever spent. We didn't have parachutes and those that weren't too sick to do it, worried. We'd watched too many of those planes come in and crash when they landed."

We were there at Camp Lucky France in the hospital for wounds and malnutrition about a week and then they seemed to have forgotten us. We sat around the camp for about a month, finally we got together and went to the commander of the company, and it wasn't long till we were on our way home. We landed the same place we shipped out from when we went overseas. I was glad to see that door way. It had a sign over that said, "Through this door way passes the best damn soldiers in the world."

I was discharged at Camp Cook, California, Dec 4, 1945. They handed me a box of Medals and believe it or not I was a little bit proud of them. I received the Purple Heart, combat infantry badge, good conduct medal and four major battle stars.

In fact, Jemmett said he didn't even learn he'd been awarded the Bronze Star for a long time after the war. "I was working in the timber in Washington when I heard they was giving free license plates to former prisoners of war," he said "when I brought my papers in to apply the guy there compared them with a list he had and said 'You've got another Purple Heart and a Bronze Star coming'". He still doesn't know what prompted the Army to award him the medal for valor, Jemmett said. "There was so many things during the war that people might think were heroic. We just did what we were told. We did things because they were there to do." said the veteran of five battle campaigns in the European theater.

He's less proud of the Bronze Star than of his Combat Infantryman's Badge, the emblem of soldiers who have fought in battle. "I know what I did to earn that," he said emphatically. Jemmett was with the 5th Army's 101st infantry. They landed at Naples and fought their way up the boot. It was a long and torturous journey, he said, marked by bitterly fought battles. I dug up about two thirds of Italy he said wryly. "Every time we stopped, I had to dig another foxhole."

He was wounded in the leg by shrapnel in one of the battles, Jemmett said, but a medic removed the pieces of metal from his flesh, cleaned and bandaged the wounds and he was sent back to the war. "When they're paying you so much money, they can't let you lay around," he said dryly. Jemmett referred to the $28 per month privates were paid to put their lives on the line for their country. His wages improved by the time the war ended; he was a corporal earning $80 a month.

When he tried to claim POW medical benefits after the war, Jemmett found there was no record of him being a prisoner. After years of haggling, the Army finally admitted in 1980 that he'd been held by the Germans from April 6th 1945 to Aug 9 1945. "They were 6 months behind in paying us anyway when I was taken prisoner", he said, "so I doubt they even knew I was missing." But it's also possible the Army didn't know because all but three members of his 200-man company were killed and the group he was with was never interned, he said.

A few years after he was home, he got a head cold and his nose became extremely sore. Searching for the cause, his doctor removed a leftover piece of shrapnel that had worked its way from somewhere in his face to inside his upper lip.

Confined to home the past two years following a couple of strokes, he occupies his time doing beadwork and often thinks about the war. "I used to think I would go back and do it again no matter what had happened to me," he said pensively. "But then I think how the Veterans Administration treats us and I don't know if I would."

Back home nothing was known but that Russell was missing in action. These entries are from Daphne's *Alridge Chronical*.

(Daphne wrote) *It is with considerable reluctance that I am doing the news sheet this week, for the first time it seems a chore instead of a pleasure. Maureen wrote us awhile back the 23 and said she had a telegram from the War Dept saying Russell was missing in action, no details at all. Today Nona received another letter from her and in it she said that the telegram also said that he was reported missing on April 6th and that a lot of prisoners were taken that day. Somehow it seems to me that nothing really fatal could have happened to our laughing, loveable, fun-loving Rusty. If any of you are at all handy at praying, there is a chance to get in some real ones. I don't think I need to add that all of us are doing just that and each in our own particular way.*

(Daphne wrote) *We are very pleased to be able to print some good news today, namely PFC. Russell Jemmett is a missing soldier no longer. Both Grandma and Frank have received letters from him and we feel certain that we all will see him in the not-too-*

distant future. As we surmised, he was a prisoner of war in Germany and we can look to hear quite some story when we see him. All of the staff of the Chronicle join with the rest in giving sincere thanks to our guardian angel, for getting him through this trying time in safety.

(Daphne wrote) *You all know by now that PFC. Russell Jemmett has been in a prison camp in Germany and that he was released, put in the hospital and is expected back in this part of the world at most any time.*

(Daphne wrote) *Rusty and the Missus are really and truly up here on their own private hilltop. Golly, Golly, Golly but Russell's story does sound like a storybook yarn. We wish that we had him right here now to prompt us on a lot of things that we aren't sure of. You know a person can assimilate only just so much of anything at a given time and all the things we could write about would be like crumbs from a feast alongside of things we might say. But first remains that we do know that he was a prisoner for 38 days and was marched for a mere 500 miles during that time, that as they were hastened out of a city, they could hear artillery fire starting at the other side and in some instances even small arms fire and that eventually the men guarding the prisoners fled on without them. Russell says that our army chased them the full 500 miles and that when they were finally found by our troops and liberated, they were way up in Austria dead beat and famished and that out of his outfit only 3 left to tell about it.*

Jim Mattson told of a man coming to see Russell years later. He was slowly starving to death on the march. He just couldn't eat. One night Russell whittled him a spoon out of wood. He looked up Russell to tell him how thankful he was. He would have died if Russell hadn't helped him.

MERL

Not sure, but this may be the last three soldiers remaining of Russell's company. Russell far right.

Les Jemmett

Leslie entered the Army Air force on Pearl Harbor on Dec 7th.

(Alma wrote) *I got to Salt Lake City to start business school the day before Pearl Harbor got bombed on Dec 7th 1941. Les had been inducted into the U.S. Army. That first morning at Clarence Plants, where I would be staying to go to school and working enough to pay my board, the Salt Lake Tribune was delivered with the big news that Pearl Harbor had been bombed and there was a picture of Les (on the front page) in his uniform signing up. I went out to the camp to tell him goodbye. Henry had brought me down the day before.*

(Alma wrote) *Les married Edna when in the army air corp. in Lincoln, Nebraska. She came home to Les's old home with baby Beverly at the same time that I was there with baby Rich, when Fred was in Texas after being drafted.*

Les served in France in the air force. He worked as a crew foreman working on the ground maintaining aircraft. The entire crew was to be transferred someplace else. On the first leg of the trip, Les was told to stay to help for a while, the rest of the crew continued on. The plane was either shot down or had a mechanical problems and all his crew were killed.

George and Les arrived home within two days. Leslie arrived the next night 1 am, he'd roused Stub Quinn who'd brought him up from Firth. He stayed just long enough to get his breath, then left for Edna and Beverly; we're expecting him back again soon, maybe hoping is the word.

Joe Jemmett

Joe joined or was drafted later and served in Japan right after the end of the war.

(Daphne wrote about Joe's experiences) *Our G I Joe went to Japan with the invasion forces. His 81st Wild Cat Division had been slated for invasion duties but after V. J. Day they stayed on as an invasion occupational force.*

Joe and two companions obtained a pass and decided to explore a small village in the interior. It was the first time American soldiers had been in this particular village and the inhabitants were doubtful of the friendliness of the visitors. As they wandered around, the people kept out of sight as if it was a dead village. However, as time passed and nothing happened, the children were unable to restrain their curiosity and were soon following them at a safe distance.

(Daphne wrote) *After a hard day at the A P O the staff was having an evening snack, the cook had secured some bologna for them and Joe was making himself a sandwich. He dropped a piece of bologna on the floor and seeing that it was dirty threw it in the coal scuttle where it landed in the coal dust and dirt. The Japanese man who had been helping around the APO was watching and made a flying dive after the bologna. He rescued it from its filthy bed and wiped it off with his dirty sleeve, proceeded to eat it in such tremendous enjoyment that it turned Joe's stomach and he lost all inclination for a sandwich. He took up the remaining bologna and threw it to the delighted Jap and left the room.*

Upon reaching Japan the G. I.'s were besieged with a chorus of "Ohio" from the Japs. Wondering just what was meant the G I's would call back "Columbus" thinking it some sort of joke. It was sometime later that they learned that what sounds like Oho to them was in reality Ohyou and means "Good morning" or "Hello." It is in fact the usual greeting. The Japanese however soon learned to shout "Columbus" at the soldiers without knowing what it meant any more than the G I's had "Ohio."

Henry Jemmett

(Alma wrote) Henry tried to join up, but couldn't pass the physical because he had broken his wrist in an initiation fight when the kids were living in Firth going to high school and had a ball joint put in. He stayed on and worked on the dry farm in the Hills trying to make up for all the other brothers.

Fred and Alma Reid, with Rich

Fred Reid

Fred and Alma were married about 2 ½ years before Fred was drafted. She had baby Rich 3 weeks after Dad was sent to basic training.

He stayed at Salt Lake for 3 or 4 days and then off to Fort Hood, Texas.

Fred was on training in Texas when they were all called together and the Sarge announced that Truman had dropped the Hiroshima Bomb on Japan and "it packed a wallop." Japan surrendered a few days later. Dad thought they didn't surrender right away and the second bomb convinced them. He thought the bombs were horrid, but if American troops had to go through Japan, it would have killed many more on both sides.

Fred wasn't released yet though. He finished training in Texas and went on to Georgia. Alma took 6-month-old Rich on the train later to join him.

Mom and Dad lived in Georgia for about a year. (Alma wrote) *I really had a good time in Georgia with my little boy and Fred all to myself, when he was home.*

Veterans from the Firth area who served in World War II, and missed out on graduation with their classmates, were given their high school diplomas in 2002. Dad graduated Firth High School with my daughter Sage.

Burial Sites

Henry and Lizzie Goddard Jemmett ------------------ Hillcrest Cemetery Shelley Idaho
Cliff and Daphne Webb Jemmett------------------- Hillcrest Cemetery Shelley Idaho
Harry and Eliza Jemmett-----------------Hillcrest Cemetery Shelley Idaho
Lois Pratt Jemmett (Henry) and Evelyn -------------------Blackfoot Idaho
Martha Carling, Leslie, Marcellus and Isaac Webb ----------------------Basalt Idaho
Edward Webb ---------------Riverside Idaho
Alma (Bill) Webb ------------- Springfield-Sterling Cemetery Idaho
Mary Ann Browning Jemmett --------------------- Heber City Utah
William Thorpe ---------------------------Brigham City Utah
Elizabeth Sims Thorpe---------------- Samaria Idaho
Amelia Thorpe Goddard -------------------Samaria Idaho
Eli Goddard ---------------State Hospital Washoe Nevada
Edward Milo Webb -----------------------along the Platte River
Caroline Owens Webb ----------------------Fillmore Utah
James and Hannah Griswold Webb ----------Nauvoo pioneer cemetery Illinois
James Clark Owens, -------------------unknown Iowa
Abigail Burr Owens ---------------------------Fillmore Utah
Adelbert (Delly) Webb --------------------Salt Lake Cemetery Utah
John Witt Carling ------------------Fillmore Utah
Emiline Keaton Carling -------------Nauvoo Illinois
Isaac and Asenath Browning Carling------------------- Orderville Utah
Johnathan and Elizabeth Stalcup Browning -------------Ogden Utah

Epilogue

If I could give you bit of advice it would be to ask questions of your living ancestors. It's very easy to keep notes on your computer and organize them under headings. Someday someone is going to want to know and you will have the answer. Oh, how I wish I could visit with Cliff and Daphne now. I have so many questions I would ask. I know now how they would have enjoyed telling me. Make sure you tell your kids and grandkids family stories. Someday they will want to know.

I have entered all my information on ancestry.com. With a click of your mouse you can fill your tree from another tree that has the same relative. It is amazing how fast a tree can get out of date, with babies born, marriages and deaths. It is a very rewarding hobby and provided me hours of entertainment.

Thanks again to my family to seeing this through to the end. I could have never done it without your help.

Sources

Jemmett, Daphne Webb. *Alridge Chronicle*
Idaho History Bingham County book Volume I 1890- 1990
Idaho History Bingham County book Volume II 1895 -1995
Pioneers Gunsmiths and Guns, Daughters of the Utah Pioneers, May 1980
To Commemorate the Orderville United Order 1875-1885 Copyright 1974
Overland Pioneer Travel, LDS website
Shelley Pioneer
Blackfoot News
"The Life and Travels of the Kid Trapper," Russell Jemmett's life story
ancestry.com
Reid, Alma Jemmett, *Along the Rivers,* 1994
Snake River Echoes 1985
Pages of the Past
Pages of unknown source that someone had copied
The Shoshone Frontier and the Bear River Massacre

www.ingramcontent.com/pod-product-compliance
Lightning Source LLC
Chambersburg PA
CBHW051511100526
44585CB00043B/2461